Silent Conversations

To Elaine

David Aylward

Silent Conversations

David Cysewski

iUniverse, Inc.
New York Lincoln Shanghai

Silent Conversations

All Rights Reserved © 2003 by David Cysewski

No part of this book may be reproduced or transmitted in any form or by any means, graphic, electronic, or mechanical, including photocopying, recording, taping, or by any information storage retrieval system, without the written permission of the publisher.

iUniverse, Inc.

For information address:
iUniverse, Inc.
2021 Pine Lake Road, Suite 100
Lincoln, NE 68512
www.iuniverse.com

ISBN: 0-595-30028-6

Printed in the United States of America

Contents

Preface xv

PART I   POEMS

Some Glitter From the Heart 3

Merry Silence 4

Tulle Fog 5

Watercolor 6

Monosyllabic Verse 7

Always Here 9

Constants 10

Eros Knocking 12

Fulcrum 14

Gull Thoughts Clustered 15

How Simple It Is 16

March Snow 17

Moonwise 18

Old Black Crow 20

Ownership 21

Rain Forest 22

Sea Walk	23
Would Ye Come Wi' Me Now?	25
London Town	26
Birthday Nod	28
We Look at Living	29
Soul Mate	30
A Short History, Sans Time	31
We Share a Script	33
Temple Days	35
To Janette on Valentine's Day	36
The Turning	37
Free Now	38
Challenge	39
First Form	40
Ocean Dining	41
The Call	42
to e e cummings	43
Where Goes Darkness	44
You See, It's Like This	45
A Time Ago	47
Earth Prayer	48
Just How Far Back Do You think We Go	50
That's a Plenty	52
There Are Others	53

Contents

Pennsylvania II 55
What Trouble We Go To 57
Night Walk, a Meditation 59
If We Are Only This 61
Faith 64
Dinner Dance 65
Listen You! 66
8:48 AM Tuesday, September 11, 2001 68
One Month Later 70
Ground Zero 72
Carving 75
Center 77
Consciousness Expanding 78
Darkness, My Mother 80
Human Being 81
Millie Came 82
Seed Centers 84
Spring, You! 85
Ancient Youth 87
Anniversary 1994 88
Awakening 90
A Fluttering of Moths 92
Alpha/Omega 93
Distances 95

Little Forms As Yet To Be	97
An Old House Burning	98
To Speak To Be	99
We Are One	101
Chicago I: The Trial Begins	102
Chicago III: Tired Walls	104
Circle, Circle, Circle	106
Ewart	107
I Celebrate the Motions of Joy	108
I Took the Day Away	109
To Ken's Fifty Years	110
March Winds	112
Menuhin in Flames	113
To Lee	114
Yabut They	115
People of Choler	117
Thrasher Dance	118
Forgiveness	119
Be Still	121
In Another Time	122
Inklings	123
Michelle	124
Perennial Granddaughters	125
Watching the Sara	126

PART II   LETTER CONVERSATIONS

On My Mind 129

Family Beliefs 132

Life and Death 134

Letter to Ken and Judith Not Far Off in Japan 136

A Letter From Me to Humanity 138

The Conversation Goes On 140

PART III   THOUGHTS AND MUTTERINGS

The Year Begins: January 1, 1994 145

Faces 147

Christmas 1991 148

Miracles 149

What's Happening 151

Desire 153

A Declaration of Autonomy 156

Eve of War—September 1990 158

Cause, Change, Create, Transform and Let Be 163

Desert Storm—The Aftermath, 1992 168

The Concept of God 171

Honor the Order of Things 174

The Day the Lying Stopped 176

Attack 178

The Enemy Game 180

A Giant's Strength	183
Key Values To Transform Our Political Conversation in the World	186
Ego and I	193
Openness	196
Addiction to Violence	199
An Opinion About Opinions	203
The World According to An AARP	205
The Importance of Being Presumptuous	208
Transition Times	210
Children of Light	213
Each One of Us Makes a Difference	215
On the Edge of Formlessness	217
So It's Not Christmas	219
War No More	222
Beachhead	224
Can We?	227
Declaration of Intent	229
Here We Are	231
The Problem of Certainty	233
Declaration for Humanity	237
The Democracy of Spirit	239
Shades	240
The Prevention and Creation of Supply	242

Contents

The Gong 244

Regarding Words 245

What Is To Be Done? 247

Specters 250

Acknowledgements

There is my dear wife, Janette, who has nudged and prodded, oh so gently, that this work be done and published. And there is Peggy Day, ever more than editor, but that, too, and a spiritual fellow traveler for going on half my lifetime. Then there is my computer tech-master, Nathan Manwiller, and then there you are, all of you with whom I have experienced and shared eight decades of Earth time. I am so grateful for your being alive with me.

Preface

This is a gathering of words. Here are poems and non-poems, mutterings. They come from a place, a center that doesn't exist in the physical, in matter, energy, space and time. Yet it is a place from which all-that-is takes form and becomes perceivable. This is a place where somethings are created from nothing.

In the course of experiencing life on this Earth since the Spring of 1923, I have come to the certainty that this place exists in each of us. We know it as a bright idea that shows up as we ponder what is to be done or we suddenly think of the word needed to complete our crossword puzzle. As children we experienced it as fantasy and play. Great religions create ornate edifices for it and call it God, Allah or Yahweh—a process which calls forth awe in us but often also calls upon us to deny our own direct connection with that center, that place from which we, humanity, give expression to our innate creative power. I would call that place sacred and acknowledge it to be a creative habitat for all, from Bach to the least articulate among us.

It occurs to me that the word Sacred rests well in that center. Sacred implies creative power, which we humans share as a gift from the Creator. It implies light and brotherhood, joy and laughter, and yes, all that is not-sacred, the awareness of which allows the Sacred to be experienced.

There are moments, oh there are moments, when this sense of the Sacred comes upon me and I am awakened and aware. Sometimes it is a small swatch of scripture such as Jesus saying, "I must be about my Father's business." Or a Bach chaconne, or Louis Armstrong singing "It's a Wonderful World." Or Edna St. Vincent Millay's "Oh God, I cried, no dark disguise can e'er hereafter hide from me Thy radiant identity…" The Sacred can sneak up and pounce at any moment. In the theater, in sports, in the grief from loss of a loved one. And often in the total aloneness of Silence.

Silent Conversations

So. I invite you to enter our Sacred place and engage with me in Silent Conversation.

David Cysewski
Summer 2003

I

Poems

Some Glitter From the Heart

In the morning of every day
you bring to me a breakfast tray
of sweet acceptance, a tender smile
a willingness to go the mile, again
to make rough edges right and
balance whatever stirred the night.
You bless the day that follows
with your loving light and
spread it out; and, as they show,
blessing all who share that glow.
This you do, and every day!
Whoever sent you to this time
had the well-being of us all in mind.

Merry Silence

Silence fills the spaces of our being here.
The two of us and our two cats
We move together among our things and selves
Cause whirls and whorls of Silence.
And as we move about we blend in Silence, dance as one.
We separate and move on among the walls
Move on among the silent rooms, through doors
And out, whirling Silence among others in our town.
We dance among ourselves and mix our Silences with those
Of cats of birds of friends and passersby.
We realize, enriched, the vibrancy,
The lighted Silent mixture of our time and town.

Merry Silence then to you!
Happy whirling through all our Silent days.

—*Silentmas, December 25, 1992*

Tulle Fog

Cool air settles gently
on the warmer waters of the lake.
Fog forms shapes and shades, rising,
silent mysteries in huddled grey groups crowded.
First sunbeams find the way through the town, tentatively,
as would a deer come to the lake to drink.
Full moon, unable to escape in the cover of night,
waits submerged at lake edge,
huge pearl undulating in a muskrat's wake.
Gull resting on calm and pewter waters mid-lake,
discovered by the sun, reflects starkly white, a
visual shout in the silence of the dawn.
Cool air warms gently in the blessing of the sun.
Fog shades and shapes disperse, muttering,
then are gone.

Watercolor

Across the lake to the west
reflecting off the rising sun
tree lined slope laid dark
with quick brush stroke,
grays now, green receding,
lake, breezeless,
awash with melding color.
Oh! How many grays there are!
reflecting this palette of only one dawn

Monosyllabic Verse

Wren house twigged, egged, fledged
Wrens now gone.
But what is this?
Toad face smiles

****

Grand he grouse
Puffed, posed
Pump on the run
She, plain and brown,
hears, sees
Says yes
Oh yes

****

Hail eggs,
full of life
bring us peace
bring us strife
Then, when our
time is past,
you bear the
the forms
our lives
have cast.

Silent Conversations

Hail eggs
so you are back
to spread old forms
along the track
those which be fore
like those which
be back
Hail eggs
I bid you,
crack!

Always Here

Poems are round things.
They are spaces that move and float
    in mind winds.
Poems are here, always here.

Trees are life urgings.
They are light things that spring, dancing
from mind soil.
Trees are here, always here.

The Earth is a round life urging
a being that pulses alive
from the nothing of space.
The Earth is here, always here.

You and I are containers of these.
incubators of space
where nothing is, yet.
You and I are here, always here.

Roundness, urgings, spaces,
incubators of spaces
poems, trees, the Earth
And we, dancers in mind wind,
springers from mind soil,
incubators of whatever is next,
We are here, we are always here.

Constants

It would be well to know this
    constantly.
That we live in rhythm with
    the universe
That you are there, with me
That music and laughter and the body game
    are pleasant reminders,
    carrying the seed of All-beauty
    which is God
That pain is not a barrier but
    a threshold to cross
That birth and growth and decay and death
    are simply dances or rhythms
    which manifest the truth
That loss and separation are only the
    blindness of ignorance
That the light we call beauty—
    which is love—is never darkened
That those motions that are seen as
    negative can be made positive in action
That hiding and avoiding that which is,
    is a game which dims, but cannot
    stop the light
That love emanates spherically and
    cannot be assigned to channels, for

Constants

     love melts the walls of channels
That I exist unseen as do you, and
     what we do is all that can be known
     of us as forms
That every cell of the universe affects
     every other
That love begets love, hate begets hate,
     waiting begets waiting, grief begets
     grief, fear begets fear
And it is action which opens doors,
     melts barriers, and opens everything
     to the light
Action and the love of one for another.

Eros Knocking

A riot of ideas within
A riot of spring outside
Myth-the whole package of
Man/Woman
The nowness of us
Commitment
Encounter
The act of creating
Engagement
Not abandonment
Commitment
Not letting go
Taking hold, wrestling.
Rage, ecstasy, joy channels creativity
The within together with
The without
The utter aliveness of mountains
The motherness of some
The fatherness of others
The laughter of trees here in our wood
The image of a wood spirit
Upon whom we have intruded
Who will accept us as we accept her.
A truce struck
The end

Eros Knocking

The promise
Not peace, more
Riot, the involvement of family.

Fulcrum

Who knows then the point of balance
The fulcrum, where the weight of
Heavy is spread throughout, balanced,
Carried by all that has gone before,
The foundation on which
The fulcrum rests?

Who knows but I,
Each and all of us?
Bent down or standing free
Released by fulcrum spread
From the weight of heavy to
The point of balance
The foundation spread,
Dug in, or,
Too much,
We tumble down.

Gull Thoughts Clustered

On the eastern shore of the western sea,
I reached out and they came to me
Clustered like gnats on a mountain trail,
Or thundering shoreward full in sail
They came to me,
Gull thoughts clustered, from out of the sea.

Gull thoughts clustered, they came out of the sea.
Thoughts familiar, reminding me
Of lessons learned in another time,
Lessons learned on another shore,
Where I reached out and they came to me
Gull thoughts clustered, and promised more.

How Simple It Is

How simple it is
This being alive
In the clearing which
Openness brings.
This being alive among the boxes
Tumbled among ourselves
Boxes all windowed and door'd,
Opening, closing
Freeing and muffling
Our angry shoutings, our singing
And our laughter.
This being alive in the
Clearing where we
Reach and withdraw,
Reach, touch and withdraw
Afraid and brave at once
To the possibilities of us.
How simple it is
This being alive
In the clearing which
Openness brings.

March Snow

The snow in our woods in early March
Is old snow mostly.
There is October snow still, crushed
To the hard frozen ground
Buried beneath the winter layers
Settling, too.

There is snow in layers
Which first came shrieking and hissing
Horizontally—stacking side to side
In drifts, creating hills and dunes and
Shapes and shadows for our eyes
To see what we put there to see.

And on moon nights full with winter
Tree trunks and shadows of tree trunks;
Twigs, broken branches echo on then off
The lumpy whiteness in startling
Black/white purity; bring simple and eternal
Messages and chuckles. Old winter
Buson on the prowl.

Moonwise

Last night
The moon circled the house
East to south to west, and called me forth
Just above the edges of the hill in back.
And her light fell full in my face
Not just once as I turned to her.
She spoke to me in silences
Of where I have been
And who and where
I am yet to be.

Be peaceful
So that I can speak to you
Word songs meant to call you forth
Word songs meant to open you
To silences deep as night
Where the moon has
Gone, and the sun
Is yet to be.

Be still
That the song you are begin
To form, that your voice come forth,
Giving form to who you are and
Where you come from; of
Deep night silences

Bereft of sun,
Of moon, of
All but your
Speaking.

Be awake
That peace and silence
Are well attended to, for they
Are universes not yet come forth
And are formable by and from
The songs you form, the words
You voice. That the moon and
Sun return in their due
Course is also true
Of you.

Old Black Crow

Old black crow
    Walks with waddling strut
Stops
    Stretches his neck
Says caw says caw
    Is answered
Re-answered
    Caws begetting caws

Old black crow
    Lies
Says caw says caw
    Says
Nothing here to eat
    Eats
Cawing and lying
    Caws begetting caws

Ownership

I do not own the fire
I do not own the song
Nor do I own the light which waits
Just beyond my reach.
Nor do I own the breath I breathe
Nor the sound of living things
Our heart beat on and on.
Nor you beloved do I own.

There's not a thing I own.
But mine it is to laugh, to cry
And mine to gyre and perne
To undulate atop the sea waves of my days
To see, see through the murk exuding from
My forgetful fear. See through to you
Oh light, to find me there.

Rain Forest

Small raindrops spread and soak
Nourish the seed and feed the root
Drip then through to join themselves
And gather among the tumbling others
Working chemistry under foot.
Drop by drop they cycle on
spreading out and gathering
to form and drip and form again
gathering, gathering fir filtered rain.
Becoming rivers, the
Dungeness and Wynooche, the
Bogasheil and Stillaguamish, the
Quilayute and Hamma Hamma, the
Queets, Elwha and Hoh.
Highways they are for small raindrops
To pell mell down then brake
To the last slow meander
Into tidal reach up from the sea.
Highways too the other way
To salmon and the harvest trout
Focused and coming home
Through tidal fingers from the sea.
Small raindrops spread and soak.

Sea Walk
To Daughter Nancy

Let us walk together,
You and I, along the beach
Laced with tidal foam
Where long sand squirts and pops
Where rock pool creatures wave and dart and scuttle
Brief universes formed and gone
Life cycles whirling between tides.

I said that I would tell you of the times before
And if you listen well, you'll hear it all
Within the sound of surf,
Where motion piles on motion. Listen.
The gull keens loud and clear
The one sound etched upon the other
Brush strokes streaking in the wind
Oh! I would have you hear it,
My friend, my daughter!

Within those sounds which we have shared
Are sounds which may not yet have come to you
I hear the sound of anchor dropped, the sudden letting go,
The clanking roar, "How does she lie?" the captain calls,
The mate's response, the paying out of chain
Slowly, till flukes dig in, winch brake is set,

And the telegraph clangs to those below
"Finished with engines."

What is it I would share with you?
Surely not these sounds inscribed in memory,
But more the act of listening I would share,
For hearing only brings what was
While listening has to do with now
And silence lies like tidal pools
Among the rocks along the shore.
Silence holds and then lets go,
Contains and promises more.

And then what would I promise you
That you would know beyond this beach
Beyond this walk along this beach?
For I have heard so many other voices in the surf,
I have,
And they are there for you to hear,
Although it takes some reaching.
Nor are their voices like our own
They form their words as ours form us,
They form their words
And crash them on the beach.

I promise nothing beyond this day.
I promise all within this silence,
Yes, within the pound of surf,
Within the keening of the gull
And foam laced squirting popping sand.
The waving cycling scuttling rock pools
Fill now with the surging tide
Fill and advance upon the beach
Where, laughing, you and I
Must scuttle back.

Would Ye Come Wi' Me Now?

Would ye come wi' me now o'er the edge o' the hill
Where th' night owl's whooo gives the chill to the spiny hairs
And stirs all manner of dreads from all of time?
Would ye come wi' me now? I wouldna' go alone
Nor be wi'out ye in the dark times coming.
I hadna' thought to leave here now
For I'd rather stay wi' ye till time for both
For then the dark may na' be so bad.
Would ye come wi' me now o'er the edge o' the hill,
Where, Earth-bound still, we can know the
Tug o' her spinning and spinning?
I know luv, we canna' abide there long
But just wee moments more.
I am near ready, then we'll go.

London Town

London town circles
and swirls
A living fresco of faces
and autos and buses.
Voices in cadences from
all the shires of the land
Languages and costumes
of the world
Alive in the spaces
among the crowds.

It is impossible not to center
here, and here
To look into that face which calls you
there, and there
It is impossible not to notice
the quick closing
of other faces,
Their struggle to shut down to you,
To be not there to you.

There are those who are open
Who look back and
see you there.
Often it is a child face, open
Or an older one at peace within.

London Town

And then that arcing occurs,
That light burst,
When Silence holds the
moment in balance.

London town circles
and swirls,
A living fresco of faces
and autos and buses, and,
Silences of Light.

Birthday Nod

I have said to you, my partner,
    zeros we are,
Within and from Zero
    and that is so.

Let that not be cause to
    not appreciate, or ignore
The value, the gift, the grace
    of our connection.

Yes, the light Itself
    moves out through each
And multiplies at our connection
    moving on out in swirls of glitter

Encompassing others,
    all others at last
Brightening, calling forth more,
Regenerating,
Gathering our children;
Zero's progeny of Light.

We Look at Living

We look at living in terms of time.
We watch it pass.
We nod and say, "How fast, how fast!"
And pick our way as the hours pile on,
While days become events,
Then, are gone.

Life itself is more a roar.
Time piles like breakers on the shore.
Life spreads out there, more and more.
We are still awhile and then pass on.
No measuring it, it just is,
As it was before.

So love, we'll let the breakers roll
Let the tides beat on
Let them ebb and flood, neap and stand
As in the center we live on
While our heart beats accumulate,
Uncountable as sand.

Soul Mate

I have been thinking, said David he said,
And what I've been thinking is this:
Thirty-one times we have celebrated this day,
Eleven thousand-plus turns of the sun.
Ever reminding us as the days became months
With years and decades coming on.
There was joy in that moment,
Our paths at last crossed in
A flaring of enough light to see
What your parents they thought
Was the birth of a daughter
Was the birth of a soul mate for me.

A Short History, Sans Time

It was into time you came
When I was at sea
It was time that enthralled us
    kept us apart.
And in time we wandered,
    each on a path
Wondering and aware of
    someone out there
Not knowing who,
    not knowing where

Some lighted urging not
    related to time
That made time seem forever
    perhaps never, we thought.
Time kept on ticking but
    something else, too
As we gravitated nearer,
    our paths at the cross
Someone was out there,
    but we didn't know who
Then you saw it was I
    and I saw it was you.

Though time still enthralls us
    we no longer allow

Silent Conversations

Time to keep us out of
    sync with our vow
To live out our lifetimes
    In touch with our Now.

We Share a Script

We share a script
A story told from all we yearned for
Throughout the years before our crossing
Where now we join together and give form to
This resting place
This energizer
This woodland center
This table set for us here in the wilderness.

Perhaps in our shallow dreams
We would be elsewhere,
You in bustling city scene
A music place, and I,
A seashore place, gulls calling to the crow
Surf pounding down, and down and down
Pulling the shoreland and mixing with it
Centering me with seaformed song.

And yet we settled here
Far from city and from seashore.
Never would we have willed it
Yet will was there in force aplenty, and
Our home exists just as though
It were meant to be a place,

Silent Conversations

A necessary place aligned for crossings
Such as our own, and nurturing them.

And then it comes to me so clear
It matters not where is our place
Nor who the others are, paths crossing ours
Sent to us or stumbling in from unseen tuggings
Where we have joined together and given form to
This resting place, this energizer, this woodland center
This table set for us
Perfect for now and for who we are.

Temple Days

Another year
A passing
We seek to hold steady
To find the day that follows the day
That follows the day and sooner
And sooner, time now racing
to find us and push us along.
Temple days, there are temple days
Days that form themselves
Form themselves as though for joy
Days that form themselves as though
Answering our question
How would you have us be?
How would you have us be the
Form for each one of us
And thus for all?
And then this silence
This still place
This laughing place
We shape together
Oh thank you.
Another year
A passing
Holding steady.

To Janette on Valentine's Day

Ach Scotty, I still call you that in my silence
For it speaks to me of how dear you are.
Comes now the wonder of how we joined our lives,
So different they were. So one they are.
Scotty! Ye gentled your being into my life
And so you have gentled me.

Aye lass! This moment just Now
Brings all that you were and are to me, dear Scotty
All the blessings we've shared!
And the gentle silent moments when we look beyond
Through loving eyes to see the very truth of us.
Ach Scotty, how dear ye are!

The Turning

The first ice crystal to form,
ceases to be what was
Now frontiersman, transformer
Ahead of his time.

Ice forms not by force
But gentled atom by atom,
H's and O's the same
But colder,

And old ones too
Slide the ice of time
As child through man
As chill through floe

Oh so gently does it,
our fluid world transforms us
Free at last to rise above it.
No more for now the storms.

Free Now

This morning I walk in a snowy land
And I let old enemy go.
I've held them close in my fisted hand
And I let these people go.
I looked upon my enemy scene
And found them filed on my blaming screen
I had them stacked with no room between
And I simply erased till the screen was clean,
I let old enemy go.

I let old enemy go, I did.
I let old enemy go.

Old time he squeeze us in squared off box
But I let old enemy go
I've held them in time and set them like clocks
And I let old enemy go

Oh I go out, free now
Free now from guiltiness
Free now from fearfulness
Free now in happiness

I let old enemy go, I did
I let old enemy go

Challenge

If you should take this step (the choice is yours)
It would be well to think on this:
Long days ahead, and moonless nights
And sadness never guessed nor wished are yours.
Infinite movement is a clashing dance,
pain a function, a part of all.
We cannot ask an atom if it hurts from
the endless movement of its universe
But watch the wave gnash at the beach
And sand the mighty rock become.

If you take this step you'll dance with time
And everlasting your rhythms twine
With rumbling quake and leaping flame
In syncopated movement fall
To rise to heights ne'er dreamed
To crash upon an endless wall
To creep in wormlike silence
To core of Earth, to mother's womb
And back to watch the flowers bloom.
Are you ready? Shall we go?
I hear heart quake, volcano roar.
The step is taken; you'll die no more.

First Form

How silent the thought that lets,
by gentle tugging, its presence be known.
Formless yet, not first-formed
into the shapes of words

I wait and listen.
Then as I speak
Silence tumbles into form
the words that speak the thing
before the thing becomes itself

Before the thing itself has time
in which to be, there are inklings
which urge us to let go needs and
hungers and all such clutter.

The promise is vast silence
underscored in the beat of drum
and something else not sayable,
never formable in a box of words.

Ocean Dining

Goeducks and razor clams
Tidal pools aclutter
Tentacles and snapping claws
Called to dine on one another
Starfish grasp with suction cups
And open clams unwilling, then
Down them rare, greedily enswilling.
Seagulls soar on wave-pushed airs
Whining cries in the ambient roar
Eating, too, of species other, between
Scudded skies and ocean floor.

The Call

So clear the call that found him here alert.
He turned to see across the green a form
Of one who called, perhaps a wave or smile?
Across the green no caller showed, not there.
Nor was there mark or motion traced by time
Nor did a twig or leaf betray one's passing.

He knew the call had come to him, alert.
That such silent calls are sourceless, do dismiss.
He'd tell you this for you to know that, "Here
Am I until I go, until I know
The source, until again she bids me come.
Yes here I am to stay alert, or go."

The crossing's yet to be announced, but soon?
Old tremblings arch, unfold, then let all go.
Time was, no longer measured by the breath,
Nor jerked by clockwork. Time paused and passed.
Lighted, rising Silence crossed the green
To him in place, alert. The call, at last.

to e e cummings

by now you
know you are
and have always been
the center of the universe
fighting or not fighting
silent alone
I mean
alone

and now you know there is
all/nothing there and you know
from the silence
from the silence
in the silence
where the tree is
before the seed is
in the silence
where e e is
before the poem is
in the silence
by now you know

—*(e e cummings died august 1983)*

Where Goes Darkness

Where goes darkness where light becomes,
insinuating itself along the edges of the day?
Darkness creeps, tucks in behind things,
trees and rocks and mountain ranges,
hides a while, hassled though, fugitive.
Escapee from the light of day.

There is an end to it, a stand is taken
The expanding encroachment of the light
begins to end at the peak of day
where the flow begins reversal
Where darkness grows and grows
As the light keeps finding a new place for itself
Being always everywhere
And unaware of other than
being it, the light itself.

You See, It's Like This

The world in time grants us now
a span of breathings which do allow
each day to pass, the familiar
mirrored in a darker glass.
Where wonder melts to silence
all that seems to be, and voices
speak, but silently.

Our breathings mark the beat
of works begun, yet not complete.
Centered ever in not yet song,
pulled by that internal come-along
that calls each dance of every day
Promising, promising, "Here's the way.
Come out, come out, come out and play."

As I enter my 80th year
It's time again to get my act in gear
to complete the work so long begun
that sits there grinning at my fear
But hold! Today is marked to have some fun
Tomorrow, tomorrow, it will at last be done.
Tomorrow, tomorrow, it will all be clear.

Never mind that the path is strewn
with not dones and never wills

that glare out there, night and noon
pieces of what might have been.
Yes, but then the sages say
What's not complete on departure day
remains with us as we rest, and then begin
Again, again and then again.

A Time Ago

It all happened.
That is so.
It happened then
A time ago.

A time ago
Is never now.
All that happened
Curves off in time
Spins out, is gone
Away forever.

Nothing out there to be rued.
Nothing to shrivel in gnarls of was.
Now was, it's gone
The same as never.
Yet still, now is;
Now forever.

Earth Prayer

Help us to see what it is You intended
When You gave us this life and
This lovely small planet. There are those
Among us who desperately feel
That others are ready to blow us apart.
Where does this come from, this
Certainty of evil?

When I look at the images
That form from their words, the logic is there
But the action is disaster. For those who are certain
That they, over there, intend to do harm,
The only course open is to deprive them of power,
To declare them anathema,
To prepare their destruction.

I cannot believe this is a choice
You intended when You gave us this life
And this lovely small planet. And yes there is evidence
To support the contention
That unless we use force they'll wreak
their intention and bend us to evil
And deprive us of freedom.

You have given us power to create
Our intention, to gather the resources

Earth Prayer

To accomplish our promises. You have given us
Language to give form to our yearnings,
You have patiently watched us as we
Lived through the distinction
That fear begets enemy and trust begets friend.

Now there are many all over the planet
Who are learning through practice
That each passing moment is open to
Choices, that all that is living is
All You created, that there is nothing omitted
For use to our purposes, that all we attend to
Is ours for achieving.

We need now a bridge, a passage
For crossing. All over this planet
We ask now the perception that will
Bring into focus that all You intended is
Ours for the choosing. That You have
Given us power to turn from our fearings
To Your Vision ever present in trust-formed clearings.

Just How Far Back Do You think We Go

"Where did we come from? Where do we go?"
She wasn't yet six when she asked me this
Eyes round open to whatever I'd say
Her face so sincere I wanted to cry.
"Where do we come from? Where do we go?
I had to tell her that I just don't know.
"I just don't know, but what do **you** think?"
She looked at me straight. She didn't blink.
"He told me," she said, "that I should ask you.
I ask you, my father. I need to know."

The words were there waiting and formed as I spoke.
I looked out the window and heard myself say:
"We were created together before there was Earth.
We are brothers and sisters who live in vast space.
We've gathered here now, it's our anchoring place.
We've got work to do daughter, and we truly need you."

Her eyes then met mine. Her smile said, "I know."
She took my hand gently and led me outside.
We walked through the meadow and down by the creek.
We were surrounded by silence and we didn't speak.

Just How Far Back Do You think We Go

I didn't ask what I wanted to know, just who was this one who
Advised her so, to ask her father as if I would know.
Yes the words were there waiting and formed as I spoke.

That's a Plenty

Stand by the Columbia River or the Niagara
Down close
Where you can sense, in your cells,
The power
    The incessant movement
        The foreverness of the waters
Flowing, spouting,
Gushing forth, filling,
In undeniable, inexhaustible plenty,
    And the great oceans!

Now. Be as are open chasms, crannies, cavities
Gorges, great valleys, to the presence, the light,
The absolute foreverness of the universe ongoing, ongoing.
Then, then! Go with it.
Then stay, open to it, let it in and through.
Know the Columbia power,
Know the mighty Niagara.
And be, still. Be still.

There Are Others

There are others
In the number of
hundreds of thousands.
They struggle with
their self-imposed
loneliness.
They will reveal themselves
as the light brightens.
And as they do the
shadows madly
dance their own
death.
So turn up the light
For shadows lack
substance
And strength is
of the light and
not of the shadow
creating walls.

This is the new season of the
light.
Turn it up, turn it up—
And know this—it is from
you alone that this can

come.
For to bask in another's
light is to create another
shadow
Walk through the grief-constructed
wall called loneliness
Into the golden Community
where each stands as one.
For this is the new season
of the light.

—*Spokane WA, June 1953*

Pennsylvania II

When the cells sing,
    vibrant with reaching
When the pole strung wires resonate,
    alive with birdsong
When the tilt of thee, Earth,
    brings the warming rays
And the tumult of Spring days
Then trudge again the still brown
    ground, seeded
Surprised here and here
    greens shouting forth
The purples and the yellows promising.
Take then the hand of the turning Earth
And walk the heavy night and
    listen to the nuptial sounds
    of ancient seeds and recent deaths.
The yellow-eyed night crowded
    with the seed sounds and the killing.
Melt then with the decomposed fragrance
    of the first warm nights.
Absorb the sweetness only promised.
Then in the hand of the turning Earth
    a fragrance you'll be
    full of dying.

Silent Conversations

And between the poles of your
    seed time and your inevitable night
A bird song you will be,
    full of promises.

—*Holtwood PA, 1965*

What Trouble We Go To

What trouble we go to,
Breathing as we do the good air
Surrounding us
Breathing, too, the vitality,
The light of us
Tides of vitality provided for us
As are the seasons of the sun
As are our days and our nights;
The passage with us,
Some coming, some going,
Of those we will know forever.
The growth, beyond us,
Of our children
Tides of vitality, free as the air
What trouble we go to
To breathe unaware

There is no emptiness
Not about to be filled
Nor dissonance
Not about to be whole
Nor completion
Not about to begin
Nor death

Silent Conversations

Unaccompanied by light
What trouble we go to
To be unaware

Night Walk, a Meditation

In times that settle in afternoons
That mark the sun's descent
When chased by shadows, beckoned onward
Shapes of ev'ning calling in the night to come
I step through doorways once again
And leave behind the day just done.
The night falls gently in the greening time
And shawls the nestlings, comforts seedlings
Envelops and permeates the fecund earth
Brings quiet as the singers cease their song.
I step through doorways once again,
Begin again the night walk long,
The night walk tracing edges of the day
Where day just past becomes the day to be,
And night seems nothing, a mere pause along the way.
I follow the silence which draws me away
From the noises that dream thoughts begin
And I loose them there in the night
Drawn to the crossing where silence joins sight.
I sink and sink further, I float on into night
I spin gently so gently into eddies of light
I float sinking, sink floating,
Become center
Become still
Become one

Become
Be
Be all
Be zero
Extend Zero
Be Tao be Zen
Be Lover of lovers
Be Light from Poseidon
Be emptiness which Christ fills
Be laughter, oh laughter
Be daytime again.

If We Are Only This

If we are only computer and bones, skin and muscles and tendons and things
If we are only pumps and plumbing circulating stuff and gurgulating,
Then what follows is crazy and makes no sense and the growling and snarling
of the dogs of war
                    In Chechnya
                        In the Congo, Afghanistan
                    In Iraq
                          In our living rooms
                              In our city streets
                        Wherever, as the news pours in.

If this is what is so about us,
then we are now all that we can be.

Not so, I say
We aren't finished
We are in a cultural adolescence

Be still a moment, see and hear with me:

At the center of each of us
At the silent center
At the constant point
At the stands of our breathing tides
At the rest points of our beating hearts

Silent Conversations

At this silent
    constant
        resting point
At this center of no thing
We know contact, connection, one to one
Where time crumples and space collapses
At the center
We are each discrete, alone
Yet by some marvelous arcing
At our silent centers we are also one.
We move out from center to live our lives
We return to center to rest and breathe
To pause a while and be together
Like seals who frolic in the murky deep
They, too, return to rocky shore to bask and yawn
                and yarp their song

It seems so clear from center
That those who hate and throttle one another
In the myriad ways of partisans and adversaries
Are simply stuck out there
Forgetful that they are
Far from center
    Far from silence
        Far from home.
What would happen if we flopped here on our Christmas rock
And yarp-yarped at them
Flapped our flippers and let them hear silent center sounds?
Could they hear the silence and remember home?
Oh to hear Saddam Hussein chuckle and
    Bin Laden to laugh!

If We Are Only This

Oh to dance the ancient desert dances with
    Sharon and Arafat

"What's that?" you say. "Chuckles and laughter?
Stamp and clog of dancers?" Then,
"What of the silence?"
That's the simple, neat fact of it. Don't you see?
Right up close to the silent center,
Even overlapping in and through it,
That's where laughter is, and music and
Dancing and simply whirling, as seals and all God's children do.
Don't you see?
Of course you do.
Pass it on.

Faith

The path shows up
As each step is taken
No cairns, no tree notches
To show the way.
Just step and realize
Step and become
Farther now than when begun.
Look back and see
It becomes quite clear
What obstructs the path
Or keeps it hidden
Is an ancient warning
"'Tis forbidden."
The path was there
Despite the fear
And now again, it faces me
I must step
Where I cannot see.

Dinner Dance

Great eagle feeds on the edge of ice.
Six crows safely distanced.
First one crow, then another
Waddle close to eagle's meal.
Eagle fluffs to twice his size.
Crows leap back, then shuffle closer
Eagle sizes down, eats his supper
Crows creep closer, closer. Then,
Fluff—and back, and do-si-do,
Ring around a meal they go.

Listen You!

Power is our birthright, simply said.
Power zaps forth from behind our eyes.
Power channels best along love lines and
    playing together in
Clearings formed of our laughter.

Power is focus plus intention times
    alignment with the universe.
Power gives forth from one individual,
    I, not we.
"We" is a diffusion of our birthright of power
Except as "we" comes forth from each one
Focussed, intended, and in alignment
    with the universe.
"We" is powerless without each one
    standing as one.

One and one aligned with the universe? Yes.
Then space is formed, time is modified,
Light is channeled, being becomes action.

Alignment with the universe?
Ah! That is what silence is about.
And centering and laughter…..

Listen You!

Call it love.
Call it freedom.
Call it who we really are.

8:48 AM Tuesday, September 11, 2001

Not rhyme, not reason
Speaks the scene
The monster cloud, last seen
Erupting from St. Helen's maw
A murderous belch from deep below
No enemy then, no one to hate
Just lingering fear
An awareness of fate
A wondering, when is our time to go.

This cloud, this devouring cloud
This time allowed
A thousand lives, then
More, and more and more
To disconnect and then let go
To tumble a moment in apocalyptic roar
To breathe again once, then,
No more, no more.

This new morning of a summer day
The collapsing towers, time stopped, stay
Etched forever on memory's screen
A wrenching reminder, that terminal scene.
We hear them still, their last moments aware

8:48 AM Tuesday, September 11, 2001

A crushing coffin, theirs to share, then
Silence calling, calling whom?
Silence calling, calling where?

One Month Later

Now time flows like magma
Its pressure spent.
Those first days of anguish
No longer vent
Just dullness now
A sense of forever.
Where Life once was
Only memories gather, only
Silent rooms and
Empty spaces
Where laughter was, and
Beloved faces.
Time grasps the scene
Slows all but the breathing,
Yet, beneath our loss, slowly seething,
Is all that remains, reminders in traces
Traces of songs, whispered endearments
Spoken together in beloved places.......
Now time flows like magma,
Begins to congeal
Creating a lesion
That time will not heal.

There is time now to think of what's to do
What healing act can at last undo

One Month Later

This smoldering memory,
This perception of pain
What lost mercy can form again
Where only Akashic dusts remain.
What is in our power to do
What healing grace can we manage
To somehow heal, transform the damage.
Lest we be doomed to replicate
The ancient echos of love and hate?

Ground Zero

Power in patterned choices
    seen in every structure, form and standard
Monuments to grandiosity amid
    glimmers of magnificence.
Twin towers rise and tumble
    rise and tumble on our vision screens, and
    we can begin to know.
We can begin to know our human power
    as it forms and disintegrates
    whatever it is we will.

Financiers and ironworkers trade hours and
    other quanta for riches not imagined
    in the minds of fellahin. Now with the mullahs
    we all see our riches crumble,
    our hours burdened for long tomorrows
Now as we all, one by one, become aware,
    become aware, at last, of the laws of balance.
Then the mullahs and the fellahin, they too,
    awakened to the power, to the results
    of the mysterious power that
    brings to balance all that forms from patterned choices.
They join us now in mayhem.

Ah humanity! There must be a better way!
Oh my Mother Earth, and our children coming on.

Ground Zero

Such a shambles comes to you, yes you!
Our thoughtless gifts from our patterned choices.
This is a feeling thing. Feel it. A vision thing.
See it. Thus we know it. This marvelous humanity
which we know we are—as all of us!
Not only we, but they too, all of us!

Can we grasp this wisp of truth to center us,
    truth spoken in times when we humans
        first snarled, "Mine, mine!" in pangs of threatening
        hunger; when we first mistook that
        brute force was power?

Truth has only been whispered, hinted at—
    to this one, open; that one, aware.
A mystery, a yearning, to ones only,
        drawn to moments and tuggings
        from silences and equilibrium
Brief moments amid the compulsion to survive.
Whispers are being heard.
Whispers accumulate.
They do. Whispers form.
Words begin to contain them and thus they pass along,
    they gather and accumulate, till now
spoken aloud and sung in choruses.
Truth not the words but
    in the speaking, in the choruses.
Not in the words—in the hearing
    of the speaking of the music of the choruses.
Truth is water filling spaces.
Truth is spaces open for filling.

Silent Conversations

So, listen family: We humans are many and we,
                All of us, are One
                And each of us is one
                Without whom,
                We, all, are lesser

That is a truth, a powerful wisp of what is so about us. Pass it on!

Carving

A block of soapstone
Held in hand.
A knife.
A singing in the
Spaces of me.
No knowledge yet
Of the shape to come,
Though it signals itself
In the motion of the knife.
We sing together, the block
And I. We consult as the
Material falls away.
We speak in languages
Spoken before words
Were formed
Languages from which
The mountains struck their pose.
We dance to drumbeat
The stone, the knife
And I.
It is so
It is
Look here
Just now
Oh yes

Silent Conversations

And this!
How could this
Not have been before?
I have known this shape
From our beginning,
Before time.
Before time held the spaces of us,
Just after soapstone
And just before I.

Center

Sphere.
Expanding.
Within, the light.
Without, lightlessness.
Within this tiny lighted globule
Weight of all the suns and planets of the galaxy
Bound together in this sphere, and floating still,
Buoyant in the lightless sea.

Lightless in its buoyancy
Desolate, companionless, containing all
A galaxy gathered into itself adrift and free
Bound too at once and limited by
Centered infinity
The source, the light
Expanding.
Sphere.

Consciousness Expanding

Consciousness expanding,
An overwhelming light
Blasting darkness
Parting the veil
Melting the boxed-in mind forms
    that block my love.
I let it happen,
    Trustingly.
My body feels this as a loss
    Feels fear
Resists the change from familiar
    pain turned down to joy turned up.
The change that brings the sharp
    rhythm of returning life.
The kind of pain a tree may feel
    from Spring returning sap
The pain of too little becoming plenty.

Hello, I say to the new scene
    before my eyes
    the new sounds signalling my ears.
Hello, I say, tasting the sweetness
    of the living water, the spirited air.
Hello I say to all the new,
    the forever new.

Consciousness Expanding

I need no longer look at what is
      through the lying filter of what was.

Nor do you, my friend.

Darkness, My Mother

There, at the moment of looking away, darkness begins
There, in that moment, the choice is cast
Where the choice not becomes no thing at all
Where the choice not becomes what never was.
There is other darkness.

Storm darkness
Night darkness of the lamented moon, the moon to be.
Darkness of blanket,
Darkness of grief thundering within the walls.
Darkness of letting go the things of knowledge.
Darkness of truths smaller than any cell.
Darkness, infinite, womb of universes.

Reach into the black,
Touch the seeds of stars.
No false light guides nor limits the way.
Feel the darkness.
Feel the black.
Feel the love from no thing but the noon of self.
Come to know the fact of the shadows,
That passing shapes are seen only in parts,
That every reflecting plane crusts a universe.

Oh darkness, my mother,
What could I know but from you?

Human Being

Human being is an image being formed.
Not a thing, not a constant, simply being
One itself.
Human being separates, becomes you and I,
He and she, parent and child, family and clan.
Nation and Humanity. Becomes a team showing
All manner of individual forms and dances
Becomes as one and one and more.
Can you see us there? Hovering as we do,
High above the fray. There we watch and
Marvel at how our Homo sapiens
Make their ways. Oh how we shudder in the horror of
These ways, then laugh and sing and marvel too
At the glory of us, one and all.
A joy in our Humanity.
Of this we sing.

Millie Came

Each of us has
Spiralled to this place
Alone,
To share a time
In soul clusters,
Vibrant, humming.
Each of us
In our own time,
We buzz away
Called to other clusters, or
Flying free,
Hankering after
Space or home,
High mountains or
The Mother sea.

Just so,
Millie came
And then she left us.

Souls leave light traces
Where they've been
Not marbled, hewn in masses.
Just gentle glimmerings
Smiles and laughter
Warm memories

Millie Came

Which ever after
Stand in time.
Just so,
Millie came
And then she left us.

Seed Centers

There is something alive
Here in the center of the word.
Where idea and meaning fall away
And open to what is left,
Only silence; empty, yet as sequoia seed
To shadow for a thousand years
The seaward slope with something living
Here, silent in the center of the word.

The center of the word
Where nothing is
Nor silence reaching forth
To find itself: another seed
Another thousand years
Shadows joining, still
Seaward sloping
Empty of idea and meaning
Again and still.

Spring, You!

Whirl
Spin in the air
Jump mightily, laughing out loud.
Roar, be a lion
Be a wolf, be a howl
Stretch the face muscles
Grimace, snarl
Mouth agape
Snap a bee
Yell ouch in laughter
Cry out in joy
Be a bee, be-sting
Buzz at the howl
Hop robin
Kill worms, swallow them
Do what seeds do
Open, erupt oh so slowly
Be squirrelly, be nutty
Be upside down
Let marbles fall
Let them roll away
Lose them, all
Don't care
Say, "Esquishtiput!"
Say "Bornglanto thrudney."

Silent Conversations

Let the tears fall
Wail, "Oh beautiful!
Och balontlifus!"
Walk out into light
Scattering shimmering light
Shout……"Bangdangliforth!"

Ancient Youth

The surf is up at Malibu
The call goes out and
To the beach the surfers come
To ride the crashing sea waves down
Or wipeout tumbling in the roar
To surface again and go for more.

The light is up at Tiananmen
The call goes out and to the Square
The free have come
To face the ancient tyrant down
Or, met with force, to bend once more
Light's notice given, and not before.

A bridgeway opened,
A connection made,
Eggshell shattered
Cocoon opened to reveal
Free beauty glowing,
Forever hidden from
The tyrant's heel.

Anniversary 1994

It all started one day and here we are
We said we would serve
We said we would grow
We said we would be open
And remain open
And listen
And hold laughter senior to
Seriousness
Our home a temple
    A place where light is welcome
    Where light mingles with our laughter
    Where light twinkles from our eyes
    The light twinkles dancing within and around us
Light bells twinkling
Blessing the temple
Blessing the listeners
All who join us in our joy
We said these things and
Pleased our futures
Our temple houses
Our lighted spaces
Our lighted years
Now decades

Anniversary 1994

A history of us growing
And no end to it
No matter what

Awakening

There is a calling
Silence formed in urgings,
Whispers, hungers
Emptinesses that dance and expand
Gyring outward
Space bound to infinity
Space bound by infinity
Father/Mother centered.

Voices saying "God" and
"Yes" and "Look again."
Beloved, loved by
Loving

Peace

Blessed silence
Long howl of wolf,
Gull cry,
Loon chuckle,
The busy silence of worms at work
Fish dance phosphorescent in the moonless sea, all these,
And this, oh this empowering thrum,
This song before the sound of it
This huge laugh,
Delight!

Awakening

Immense thank you
Surges and fills
All shadow gone.

A Fluttering of Moths

Let us now end this mad cycle
Hate transmitted, formed by fear
Every moment ringed by danger
Unseen, hinted at, enemy, stranger.
Alien customs give us to wonder
What dark intentions lie under cover
Perhaps alien muttering signifies
Their friendly gestures may be lies
Aimed to take us by surprise.
Beware, beware,
Enemies, enemies everywhere.
Cloaks and daggers
Complete with leers
Sidelong glances
highlight fears.
To that add a daily dose
Of presidential thumps and scoldings
which bring the frightened to reduce their holdings
To lumps in mattresses and hollowed moldings
What madness this is to clutter life and
Bristle with angry froths,
Rife with hubris,
Draped with coded holy cloths
Threatened only by a
Fluttering of moths.

Alpha/Omega

The shapes of tomorrow
    solidify today
    concretize, take form
    essentially the same
    as it has always been
Footprints in time
    backward and forward
    as far as we have been
    and are to be
    each footstep varied
    slightly to seem the same
Striving, striving
    holding forth and altering
    until every form solidifies
    and what was shimmering,
    lighted, dancing, comes to rest
    and solidity, stasis, reigns.
Now there are inklings of a pathless route
    once obscured by puzzlements
    imaginings, riddles,
    which, when cleared away
    mean nothing now, nor ever
    just as it was millennia ago.

Silent Conversations

Mean nothing though
    blood of generations
    continues to spill, to ooze,
    to coagulate on ground hallowed
    by hollow mouthings of souls
    in changing shapes of enemy
Poets howl, protest,
    make words to approximate
    such grotesquery, and failing,
    howl the more and miss the dance,
    the shimmering, wordless,
    lighted dance ever calling for us
    to turn that way.

Distances

Distances containable
In geometric patterns
Composed of closeness
So far away.

Distances,
Space within released,
Freeing us to touch,
To dance our time away.

Distances lied about,
Called barriers; thus we clutched.
Yet space itself we formed
By reaching until, like this, we touch.

Ah, spaces of our reaching
Distances for our dancing!
Our very closeness thus composed
Of spaces we have formed.

So say goodbye or say hello
Connected we orbit, so,
Around around our planet go
Creating now this ancient glow.

Silent Conversations

So share we laughter
And between us pour
Careless glitter of space and time
And listen! Mother Silence at our core.

Little Forms As Yet To Be

Measure a year by the ideas that dawn
    that come as mutterings or books or music
    forms new and challenging, or
    so familiar as to tear apart their permanent places
    and scatter them like so many leaves in vortex dance
    not yet sogged down by the solstice storms.

This vortex, this right now storm I chose to ride
    to the edge of time, so I saddled it up and leapt aboard
    and pell mell thundered past open fields and woods alive
    with unseen forms that breathe and thump
    and call softly to each other of my passing,
    a danger not from my intention but because
I am of them who thump and breathe and
    fire away, ending the breathing randomly
    of forms just seen at the moment of their ending.
Old uncles and wrinkled grandmothers last seen
    breathing in the same old way as in forever
    Suddenly, for it's always sudden, the breathing stops.
Random becomes specific, the polling of this
    station ended. And it didn't get said, not all of it.
    But oh how fast it goes.

An Old House Burning

The strong man's hands have gone with the laughter,
    the work done.
Not seen in the flame,
The mothers and daughters, nor their dancing,
Nor heard in the rising smoke
    the rustle of them nor their tears.
And as the walls succumb to the flame
Space remains,
But never emptiness.
And even as the ashes cool
    the surrounding fields return.
And in the silence—
No laughter, no weeping
    no laughter, no weeping—
Only life sounds,
The sounds of forms changing.

To Speak To Be

To speak to be is
To open
Out
And in

To speak to be is
To allow the tautly stretched
Membrane I wear
To let go of itself and
Be no more

I stand then vulnerable
And powerful
In the silence
Where language forms
Where language slips down the ways
Where language is launched
Where language is outfitted
And takes to sea
With the tides and winds

To speak to be is
To plow forward and forward
To rise and fall
To rise and fall
Into the soft and forever swells

Silent Conversations

To speak to be is
To scatter light in glowing globules
Along my side
And in my wake
And witness the cresting sea tops
Glowing in return

To speak to be is
To shudder and to tremble
Held—and then released
To pound down and through
The gale-wrought sea

To speak to be is
To form what is before it is
To say it is so
Just as it is so
To move on forward into
What is formed
Exactly as the form takes shape

To speak to be is
To shake it off and move on
Yes

To speak to be is
To shake it off
And move forward

To speak to be is
To reveal with laughter
That this is all we have ever done

We Are One

This is the same land
Yet our sea-roiled borders
Protest this, froth and thunder,
Knowing the fact to be,
Beneath the surging barriers
The lands of Earth are one.

You and I, brother,
Are the same man,
Ego-formed borders
Protesting the difference. Yet,
Beyond the bone-formed talking things,
The men of Earth are One.

Chicago I: The Trial Begins

The trial begins in the
    chatter of evenings
    endless
The walls rebound the
    sounds of us—
No noise—
We form the noises of
    Fridays and Saturdays
As it has always been.

The trial begins as
    the compass forms
Finding the center of
    Itself—
Disturbed by the mountains
    and gravities of self
Yet centering, truly centering.

The trial begins, you know,
Where the words form and
    crash in thunders—
Foaming then to whispers against
    the selves
The rock of selves we've
    formed.

Chicago I: The Trial Begins

The trial begins at the
    edges of our chatter
Where the walls wither and
    totter
Where the walls lean at
    last on emptiness.

Chicago III: Tired Walls

Tired walls
Brick flying
Shards of my silence
    Glittering in the day.
I don't know you.
I don't know your place.
Blood is sticky
    and it cakes in cloth
Shirt stiff with blood
To stand—a stiff shirt;
Shards of our sobbing lying there.
Man—oh Man! What is this rumbling?
And what is the hot laughter?
And who can sneer the most?
Who is laughing—
Who is soaking his shirt—
Who is sneering?
Whose shards shatter like laughter
And glitter useless in the day?
My hand is open
My hand is a fist
My hand is open
My hand is a fist
My hand is open—and reaching finds pain—
My hand is a fist—and smashing finds pain.

Chicago III: Tired Walls

Tired walls and brick flying
Shards of hot laughter
    Glittering in the day.

—Chicago on the day M. L. King was shot

Circle, Circle, Circle

Ever winding through the knotted fabric
    of the thoughts of others
Not knowing there is a way out
Not wanting to know.
Thinking that energy of life is a gross and
    pushing thing, and that only.
Pushing while protesting the pushers.
Creator of an environment of enemies

For such as these, peace is death.
For such as these, death is peace.

Ewart

He has at last put down the loads he carried
The bundled shapes, the puzzlements.
Fear bought burdens, bundles of them dropped
And left beside the trail, while those
Who loved him sought to find him where
Only bundles, empty now, remain.
What he had feared is there no longer.
What he'd thought was heavy death is weightless now,
Is lightness, laughter lifted yet solid as certainty.
Looking back he sees them weeping
And he wonders at their grief for him
Now free, now risen laughing from the stage.
Would that they too know and, laughing,
Speed him on to love, there waiting in the light.

I Celebrate the Motions of Joy

I celebrate the motions of joy
I speak of the songs from us
I center on the quiet balances
And know, oh how quietly,
How quietly we dance.

I dance now, the center of us
I sing and expand within and without
And sing—oh sing I, and shout

I Took the Day Away

I took the day away
The space remaining a tunnel left in time.
From above, from the outside,
    the day was never there.
That is how to use the anchors.
That is how to remain unmoving
    in the surging tide.
That is how to be dragged down,
    engulfed and drowned as the waters rise
    and anchor flukes dig in.
That is how to hulk hollow haunted
    on the sea abandoned sand.
That is how to gather sea shell and space fragments and
    leave shards of what was,
    no longer there.

To Ken's Fifty Years
In appreciation of his humanity

Up from the cities
From noise and strife,
He came seeking a better life
A place that would include
one day a partner/wife
He walked the woods of the land around
and he listened to every Silent sound
And then, at last he knew he'd found
The very place for them to be.
In due time she did arrive
and together now they do strive
to enhance, add to, all alive.
It's now the end of his fiftieth year
And in all that time it becomes quite clear
He's put to silence the native fear
within which most huddle in lives dull and drear.

As partners now they till their soil,
weed, hoe, plant seeds in constant toil
Do that work when it is light
They then tuck in as the sun lets go
and they allow all outdoors to spend the night
in the ancient ways that creatures know
Leaving, too, the green stuff growing, row on row,

To Ken's Fifty Years

full with nutrients which then go, to feed
those who have come to know such is their need.

As the seasons change the partners turn
to another earth, the clay,
from which his hands give birth
to forms and shapes and spaces
that then contain steaming soups and stews,
fruits and melons, flowers galore
All containing traces from their gardens,
from their toil, which then go forth as pots and
platters in shapes and colors, which by some magic
speak of all that matters from the endless cycling
of toil and soil.

So now he stands, farmer, once squatter,
King of his hill, and—God help us!—
a hairy potter.

March Winds

March winds blew my love away
And in my chest this sadness locks
Never to be known again or felt
Only hidden sigh, this hunger which my laughter mocks.

Yes, your song is pleasing to my ear
Gently tapping at this wall of rock and lime
As the puny chisel of the tide
Crumbles continent and clam shell, in time.

You'd have me live in rhythm with your heart?
To flower the garden of your living?
How can this be when all my consciousness
Listens for the stilled beat, no longer giving.

Menuhin in Flames

Menuhin in flames
    burn furiously
Beethoven on ice
    freeze silently
The songs of men in holocaust
    growl hoarsely
The clays of earth bake
    to ghastly glaze
No poppies now
Return to no home
Only now—
    The living ones—in precious
Twos and threes

To Lee

A birthday nod to my daughter

Among the spaces that travel
    with me
The Lee space sings
    always.
And just now—the birthday time—
Lights flash with the song.
Yes, the Lee space flashes
Leeful—memories and nows
    commingled.

I saw you first this time.
At once.
Old friend.

So what's a year or two?
Or noises—what are they?
They pass.
And only spaces matter

    Flashing

        Singing

            Present.

Yabut They

I give you a puzzle
    that, come what may,
The very presence of which
    causes one to say,
This moldy mantra,
    "Yabut they, yabut they."
When it is suggested
    that our world could be better
If we exited the boxes
    with which we fetter
Our innate desires to
    laugh, dance and play,
We mumble instead,
    "Yabut they, yabut they.
Yabut they won't let us
    they'll put us away
They'll call us witches
    and burn us alive
They'll stop us and hound us
    if we dare to say,
"Open and look,
    there's a better way."
Justice is a word that is
    often heard

From those who would retaliate
    for past evil done.
Such use of that word is
    just so much *merde*
When it sanctions more violence
    more murderous fun.
Action/reaction is
    the way of the world
In return for a missile
    A missile is hurled.
And a tooth for a tooth is
    counsel long given
To activate which
    we have been driven
To call forth the Gods of our
    days in the cave
When we knew no other
    nor could imagine other ways
Than that balance be wrought
    by battle long fought.
Oh ye ancient of days
    ye ancient of ways!
Moldy the mantra
    that echoes in time
That holds us bound firmly,
    keeps us in line
As we mumble and pray,
    constricted to say,
"Yabut they, yabut they,
    yabut they."

People of Choler

The Cardinal red and the blue Blue Jay
Contrast bright against winter grey
Aggressive, crotchety
Given to fits, ever fussing in familial snits
These eruptions appear to do no harm, and
Amuse this one, well fed and warm

Thrasher Dance

Just barely, there! Flash of russet wing
Gone? No….there! still as stone.
I wait. He waits, gone in fallen oak leaves
Among lilac brush, not yet budding in the spring.
Again he waits, the listener. I wait, watcher barely breathing

Quickly then, on the ground, a great thrashing.
Fast with feet and bill, oak leaves tossed in furies
To reveal bird joys in the mulch below.
Such a ruckus! this thrasher feeding dance.
Again he pauses. Disappears in stillness. Fed for now.

Nothing could have pleased me more,
This soggy spring morning unless
Perhaps an elephant, standing tall.

Forgiveness

Whatever way we turn it
What was no longer exists
Until called upon.
It has its being
In facsimile.

        ****

Conjure is a good old word.
We conjure up an appearance,
An apparition from the past
Or any imagined time
And call it now; a lie empowered
By our speaking

        ****

Forgiveness is operating now
With the screen and projector
Shut down.
I mean the facsimile machine is
Silent.
Gone.

Forgiveness is seeing what is so
And knowing that as choice.

****

The light perceived in facsimile
Is a false light. A reflection.
Cold. Actually false light is to
What is so as shadows are to sunshine
Or a grimace is to a lover's smile.

Be Still

Be still
That the song you are begin
To form, that your voice come forth,
Giving form to who you are and
Where you come from; of
Deep night silences
Bereft of sun,
Of moon, of
All but your
Speaking.

Be awake
That peace and silence
Are well attended to, for they
Are universes not yet come forth
And are formable by and from
The songs you form, the words
You voice. That the moon and
Sun return in their due
Course is also true
Of you.

In Another Time

In another time the grey mist
Whispered tomorrow and tomorrow.
Afraid, we clutched only the day
And refused to answer.
Yet eye to eye we caught the
Meaning of the lights and shadows,
Reverberated them and laughed.
How the laughter echoed!
Time against time.
And the round moment which was ours,
Was it seed, or was it gem?
Was it tomorrows, or only yesterdays?

Inklings

I have spoken of a place
    where poems have being,
Poems yet to be formed into
    words of the time.
Then there are inklings.
Like fireflies, inklings light up momentarily,
    etch themselves on soul stuff, then seem to go out.
Poof. Gone. Like never were, but are now, forever.
Inklings connect to inklings of others
    unseen and unheard by us;
    we who are time bound, space locked, and focused.
In the dance of wave become particle become wave,
    we forget these many mansions where inklings accumulate,
Where forever, just now, the world gets brighter.
We forget all but the inklings.

Michelle

Every summer brings a new Michelle
Another year with more to tell.
And taller, too, but there is more.
It's in her eyes, something new
As though a knowing door had opened
Now comes forth, Michelle anew.

Each autumn day when summer's done
And only memory holds the fun
Of watching her become that single flower
Like no other, my daughter's daughter.
Shows more and more that unique power
That ignites joy in everyone.

Perennial Granddaughters

When summers come and the flowers bloom
They come to our home
Or we to theirs, it matters little.
For there are always laughing hugs
And other catching up to do.
With year long growth and learnings
coming forth
The child in each urging to be grown.
We say not all grown, not yet.
There's still time for that.
We know what they don't know
Or have forgotten.
Girl child becomes woman
Quite soon enough.

Watching the Sara

Lightning bundled moves
In all directions, all at once
It sparkles, crackles, changes, causes,
Struggles, forces outward into
Boundaries, barriers
Bodies all boned, muscled,
Given to wording things
To contain the lightning
Bundled as Sara

—*After a week with granddaughter Sara
2 years and 4 months old.*

II

Letter Conversations

On My Mind
Letter to My Cousin Dorothy 8/96

It was great to receive your letter! You and your brothers are often on my mind. "On my mind," that is an interesting phrase. To me that means that an image or a sense of your presence in my world flashes on my inner video screen. Unlike the television in the living room, this device of the mind is more than visual and sonic, for it contains emotions and memories and regrets and joys and love. So, as I said, you and your brothers have been on my mind and now, addressing this letter to you causes the inner video screen to light up and here you are. Here we are. I say that as I write this, you are experiencing contact with us here in our small town and your video screen is right now glimmering with our presence.

This awareness can be just a glimmer. It can be conceptual and not perceptibly detailed, but I say we connect and that we communicate. Even separated as we are, by continental geography, we certainly engage in what most of us believe are one-way conversations. I happen to believe that these inner conversations are two-way and often are more akin to conference phone calls, with many others involved. I often become aware of the fact that as I go about operating a Homo sapiens creature in such a way as to survive in the physical universe, I am also engaged in these mental conversations and "conference calls." Letters and phone calls help me focus and my conversations become more, what?....real? But they are gradiently the same process.

As I go about living here in Wisconsin I engage almost continuously in a world-wide cultural exchange. This is the inner conversation I have been writing about. And I have the gall to propose that human beings, me and thee included, influence one another by our inner conversation and each of us thus has the power to change, even save the world. There are those who claim that Ronald Reagan "won" the cold war by engaging in a bullying conversation with others he declared to be evil. I say that millions of people of good-will tired of the snarling and posturing of the war hawks in all countries and began to connect in a worldwide conversation of peace and sanity and good-will to all.

I received your letter yesterday and read it, as always, with great pleasure and a strong sense of connection with you, and your brothers.

See how that works? They didn't write a letter but they joined in this conversation, too. Are they aware of it? I really don't know, but I like to think it, i.e., to project them and you on my screen, even as I write this.

Between the time when I read your letter and now as I re-read it I have carried on a conversation with you and myself about your question, "Is God still working for you?" First, when I said that God "works for me" I did not intend to imply that I thought of God as some kind of servant or magician or genie, granting wishes. What I intended to say was that I have chosen to operate in my life as though there is a central creative power at work in the universe, and every cell, every particle, every creature, every planet, sun and galaxy, all operate in an ultimately orderly system I choose to call God. I have found that it "works" for me to operate from that base.

Once, when I lived in Pennsylvania, I was invited to a Christian Business Men's luncheon. There I heard testimonials about how Jesus helped this one sell more Cadillacs than ever before, or helped another cut a big real estate deal. Now, I believe these gentlemen sold a lot of Cadillacs and cut big deals, but I did not nor do I now believe that the Jesus of the Sermon on the Mount was involved in the magical way portrayed in the testimonials. However, I think this universal creative power does respond to the creative thought of every human being all of the time. I also think that humanity, all and each of us, is experiencing the outworking of our aggregate creative thought, our world-wide conversation.

You said in your letter that you liked the idea that we are all related to one another and then went on to relate that to our biological linkage. I say, yes we operate in the physical universe as Homo sapiens, or as a friend calls us, Homo-saps. We are linked genetically back in time to the mud and to the great oceans and to the murky eons of cellular progression. But that is our physical creature, a creature that still jumps in fear at noises and growled threats as though about to be eaten by something huge and fanged and yes, evil. It is this creature which responds to warhawk projections and the mutterings of hunters and warriors all bemedalled, and the fife and drum of battle and football. Yes.

But I say that I am the operator of that creature we call David. I and my family before me and my civilization and my awareness and my good will which comes from something other than the flee or fight genetic reality we share as Homo sapiens. I am a human being and am therefore more than the reactive creature I tow along with me here on Earth. I am more than David. I am a mind. I can create almost literally something from nothing.

An idea is nothing that can be measured but the Sears Tower and the Taj Mahal were once ideas. I can do a lot of other stuff, too. I can harbor ill-will and resentment about events that happened in the past and can get my Homo sapiens and thousands of others so riled up that they go on killing sprees, even today, when to so behave is insanity. And I can listen to the Great Teachers. Jesus, Buddha, Muhammad, and others, down through history, perhaps even before our present written history. Even now, there are Teachers who would have us forgive one another and to experience the release that can be enjoyed by everyone of us if we acknowledged that we are human being, now, and not these silly Homo saps that we mistakenly identify with.

Dorothy, that is how we are all related. We are human, being. The world we are experiencing is one that we, human being, created in the past and are right now engaged in creating toward the future. As human being, right now, this very moment, is the focal point of our power to create. The conversation, inner and outer, that we choose to engage in, now, is our focal point of power. It is idea and therefore nothing. And it is our future.

You say because of the war-torn consciousness extant in our world it is obvious that almost no one believes this which I have been saying. That is because we carry on our conversation with little appreciation of our creative power. We think the world according to television, political rhetoric, gossip and other ugliness is all there is, and thus we resignedly and cynically use our creative power to perpetuate craziness. We are related to one another. We influence one another. We create our future. What we are experiencing is what we created. Forgiveness is not only necessary to our survival, it's fun and empowering.

There! No, I haven't been writing lately. Thanks to your letter I just wrote some deeply felt thoughts and I send them on to you. Don't say you don't understand them. Just read them and hold them open to the creative process, which is an attribute of all of us human beings. It's the poor old Homo-sap that is so easily stunned by thinking, by trying to be a human being.

You say that you are still in your atheistic period. All I can say to that is that some of my best friends say they are atheists. You of course are one of our best friends, plus you are a sharer of the world conversation with us and then there is the fact of our being blood cousins to boot. So go ahead, be what you will.

You have our love, permanently. And that includes the whole universe.

Family Beliefs
Letter to my cousin Dorothy

You speak of my writings as deep. That could translate as profound, and if that was your meaning I modestly demur. But perhaps by "deep" you actually meant obtuse. Don't worry—others have said the same thing, and I am working on it. My brother Leon would often ask why I was always digging into things, going to "weird" seminars and work shops. My Dad, too. "You read too many books!" he would say—Holy Mother, the Church provided **his** answers, so why not mine?

The way I look at it is that each one of us is on a journey from clod to God. There are times when we are just poking along, content with things as they are. There are other times when we sense a great yearning and we reach out our empty cups that they be filled. These are the times when we find ourselves at our personal frontiers and strive to move on out toward what? The kingdom? Camelot? I prefer to see it as the Light, and the process one of increasing enlightenment. In my vision of this, no one is excluded, even bad guys. They are just looking backward. Actually, it's not my call.

I appreciate the news item you sent and I concur with the writers. Ideologues and fundamentalists who would force their dogmas down our throats are true terrorists, never mind whether they be Christians, Jews, Muslims or whatever. Common old everyday terrorism of the flesh, bombs and all, can be more easily countered than the terrorism of the mind. Warped, brainwashed minds can generate hatreds "unto the seventh generation." It can be very discouraging unless one remembers that minds can change by the simple flick of a choice.

You asked if my folks were strict Catholics. My dad was a Catholic to his last breath. He died on the spot at a Knights of Columbus Convention, with 250 priests there saying the rosary as he took off. My mother was not a church person. Her mother was a member of the Congregational Church, and Mother, of course, had to convert to marry Dad. She was not a religious person, but she was

Family Beliefs

a thinking person on her best days. She had much of the sensitivity that is found among the Irish. Her father was a hard-drinking Irish railroad construction contractor. The fact that mother was not really a Catholic, and that dad was born one and believed to the core, affected the three of us kids by not tossing us into a belief box where we questioned nothing. I doubt if my brother ever saw the inside of a church after puberty. Marion became a Christian Scientist. And I? Well, as Emperor Jones sings, "It's a me, it's a me oh Lord, standing in the need of prayer, It's not my brother, it's a me, oh Lord"…like that. There is something there. And, yes, I want it. But I'll climb in no belief box, not "where the Light don't shine."

Life and Death

From an April 1999 letter to my cousin Dorothy Askin

You ask if I think that life and death cannot be separated. I have come to feel that death is a natural function of life. It is as real to me as day following night that this citizen called David will someday no longer live visible as a Homo sapiens. David will have died. The one who operated David who refers to himself as "I" who was invisible while connected to David, remains invisible to five sensory perceptions after David has been put aside. This being says of himself "I am." I am, with or without a body. My body died. I am. I am a part of Life. I am here where I always was and will be. I live now, which is always. Whoever says "I am" is also a part of life, with or without a body at the time.

This is neither a new nor radical idea, for it can be found at the core of much of the sacred writings of humanity. It simply means that there is much more to our human involvement with life than we can perceive and know via our five physical senses.

I think it was the scientist/philosopher Aldous Huxley who referred to the recurrence in time of this body of ideas. He called it the Perennial Philosophy. Wherever it does show up in a culture it serves to turn the attention of the people of the time toward civilized knowledge, the arts and sciences and civilization in general and away from the superstitions and religious dogmas of their time. So far in known history this turning up of the Light energizes the people and as a result art and science and invention flourish until, as in other times before, the philosophy is altered under the control of a self-appointed oligarchy or priesthood. Then the philosophy becomes the means of the priesthood's control over the people. Then the light dims and what was dancing and flourishing in the culture begins to gel and solidify and becomes other than what was brought forward by the bearers of the light.

Life and Death

I think we are in a time when the light is turning up again. I acknowledge that nothing I have said here is supportable by five sensory evidence. But poets and actors and dancers and others in the quiet of their own living spaces are speaking from this multi-sensory viewpoint. As, in fact, many always have. I see it everywhere except in the five sensory media to use Gary Zukav's terminology in his powerful book *The Seat of the Soul*. What I have been saying is reality from the perspective of the multi-sensory personality. For us who struggle and suffer the aches and pains of our bodies, we think our bodies are who we are. We know, therefore, that our lives began and will end. We worry and sweat over the possibility that we might not survive when, to the "I," who each of us really is, survive is all we can do. How's that for a laugh? A truly cosmic joke!

You asked, lo these many lines of words ago, do I think that life and death cannot be separated. My answer is yes, they coexist. All the words preceding were my attempt to pick a logical path to my answer.

Janette and I wish you well in your aortic valve adventure. We think that at the very center of each of us is a quiet place, a lighted space, discrete and private, yet it is where we all are connected to one another and are truly one being. From that space we will think of you as health, strength and vitality, which, from the multi-sensory paradigm, is the way that it is. Or you can call it God. Or love.

Letter to Ken and Judith Not Far Off in Japan

What can we do with the spaces that are left when friends move on and away from ready contact? One thing we can do is to build a kind of shrine, a creche-like mental structure toward which we point or genuflect and mutter silent mantras, like "We miss you" or "We wish you were here."

And then we can embellish the shrine with plastic flowers, the kind that go with missing and wishing, yearning for what was, and other past-time silliness. We can do that and pretend that we are thus renewing contact when, in fact we are attempting the impossible, trying to create a permanent present out of past realities that are even now spinning off, spinning off into space.

Now I ask you, why do we do that? Well, I say that we do that because we are either just learning or are relearning certain basic truths about how we are in time. One thing certain is that enshrining the past brings no contact. Making structures out of past events does not bring them back to life. You two are there somewhere and we two are here somewhere and if we attend to shrines we will miss the happy fact that contact is forever and forever is right now, so hello again! We miss you not, for you are here right now as I write this, and now again as you read this, never mind considerations of time and space. Shrineless, we are now timeless. Timeless, we dance, make pots, write poems, bow the fiddle until the very firmament becomes unglued and we live, by God. Yes! By God.

What's to say? I walked by one of the bookcases in our house and a small volume of Krishnamurti—*Think on These Things*—said "Ahem" and lighted up, you know, as the next book to attend to always does. Of course Krishnamurti then makes me feel sort of silly like when he asks me to consider why I read this book when my real purpose is to live a life in complete rebellion. No, not angry fist-shaking-snarling-blaming-attempting-to-change-things rebellion. Rather the kind of rebellion whereby I can pause within any passing moment to "look at the stars or delight in the whispering waters…or the dance of moonlight on a rushing stream or watch the flight of a bird." The complete rebellion of being silent, peaceful, dynamically at rest.

Krishnamurti does things like that to me. He picks me up by my feet and shakes me so that my wallet and change fly out and away and I become empty and laugh out loud and be free.

A Letter From Me to Humanity

Dear Fellow Humans,

The time has come for me to say some things to you. I say them to you because you are my Brothers and Sisters. I am finished now with the companion experiences of being sorry for you, for parts of you and that most important part of you; myself. I am finished, too, with that noisy period of seeing those antics of yours and mine through tear-occluded eyes, the tears so often of loss, or derisive laughter. It is the end of laughing at you and myself. Finished too is the fighting of you by me and me by you.

The secret is out. I can fight only myself. For if I bomb any city it is my city I bomb, and the bodies that lie crushed in the rubble are murder/suicides. I am finished too with the endless task of working for the benefit of someone or thing or force, other-directed and requiring obedience. Not idea, nor goal, nor victory, nor money, nor company, nor individual, nor ownership, nor power, nor the lie of security can achieve my allegiance. For the truth is now revealed, secret only because of its simplicity, that I can only work for myself and for you, my Brothers and Sisters, whether my work is to build or to destroy.

Being finished with these things by which I have related myself to you as friend and enemy does not mean that I am no longer here, or no longer related to you. In fact it means that I am at last here with you and only now acknowledge that as fact. As to my relationship with you, I am as related to you as I am to myself. And because of this fact I would know myself better. In truth I must then know you and you must know me—as I am, as you are. Through no action, through no idea, through no form except now, as it is.

And thus is begun that first and last philosophy, the first and last world association of humankind which is to be called Ism. The practice of Ism is Isanity. He or she who aligns with the Isanity of Ism will be designated Isane and thus entitled to all of the privileges of citizenship. There are to be few rules. For example:

A Letter From Me to Humanity

1. At least once each day one must look at another human being and accept without judgment what one sees, however unlike yours another's reality seems to be. Implicit in this look is an acknowledgement that there is much more to that person than is perceivable by the five physical senses.

2. At least once each day, and for a period of not less than two minutes, one must consider the motion and tone of life around one with no assignment of good or bad or right or wrong. Simply be here now and look without thinking. Just look, take it all in. As it is. Include as much of what is, seen and unseen, as can be accommodated in two minutes. Remember, no thinking. It will do no harm to, perhaps, smile. If people inquire why you are smiling, well, tell them you are Isane.

3. Conversations which flow from the above practices have the potential to be productive of creativity and tone-raising consciousness, even joy. Of course, with joy you energize the space you are in, including everyone and everything in it. With joy, lying and other self serving alterations of what is so, simply become impossible.

It's really very simple! That's all there is to it!

The Conversation Goes On

One of the musts for us when we visit Seattle is to visit a couple—two of our forever friends. He is a close friend from high school. They are bright, loving people of good will, encumbered as so many truly intelligent ones are by a profound pessimism about the human condition. They have difficulty with the fact that, in their view, I don't have a full string of fish. Why? Well, I am not as pessimistic as they. As an almost ritual part of our get-to-togethers we respectfully review the status of this disparity of view. I should add that she is a practicing Buddhist and he takes a resigned yet dim view of that and of my references to what I choose to refer to as our being sibling children of the Creator. I feel that I understand where he is coming from because that is where we both were in high school. (With some chagrin I just now realize that I have been assuming he now holds the same views as we did then.) My friend returned from WW II and continued his formal education. I returned from the war and managed to become randomly self-educated. That makes a huge space for decades-long conversation, it seems to me. What a blessing. After one of our visits to Seattle I sent them the following letter in which I attempted to clarify my thoughts.

Look! I don't want to be foolish. I am no Pollyanna nor Pippa. All's not right with the world. But I still choose to take this stand.

I hold that there are perceptible motions and signs that we individual citizens, one by one by one, are beginning to recognize that we, each one of us, has a terrible yet wondrous creative power. We cause what we experience in the world. We experience what we cause. You may well object, citing such examples as the thug wars in Bosnia, Kosovo, Serbia, tribal chiefs in Iraq, teen gangs wherever, divorces, drug lords, Oklahoma City bombs and bombers, major tectonic plate shifts and shudders, AIDS, NRA, racist and "Patriot" militia….topped off with, "All right Dave, what did you and I do to cause those disasters?" Most of us turn away, mutter, "Ain't it awful," and deny our ownership. Denial is a caused action. Refusal to confront discomfort and forgetting to exercise our ability to

The Conversation Goes On

rise above cynicism are choices, made individually and collectively. And when one or another of us, or masses of us, do confront some disastrous turn of events, usually it is too little, too late. We seem unable to think of any explanation but blame of "them, over there." This is followed often by skillful and violent punishment of our chosen "them." Or by reason of the sheer magnitude of disaster going on as in earthquakes and floods, wars and massacres, we are left with little but the opportunity to display our barbarity and our magnificence, or the numb dumb proclivity to succumb like the turkeys we too often become.

I propose that we humans are at work in a grand scale progression from clod to God. It is abundantly clear that the population bell curve peaks closer to the clod end of the scale, a fact which I think accounts for most of the daily news and media "entertainment." I do cause my individual place on the scale and thus I contribute to the weight and direction of motion of the bell curve. So, you ask, why in hell should that be cause for any optimism? Geez, don't you see? Each one of us contributes to the direction of motion of the peak of the bell curve by our every thought and act. By every word that proceedeth out of the mouth do we influence our world. Because that is so, I believe we can't afford to lose the positive influence of people of good will such as you two friends because they feel so strongly at this time the ill will and the danger in the world.

And I take comfort in the thought that there have always been great men and women in the world, apparently just enough to keep us from wiping ourselves out. Great men and women who spoke great thoughts. Great men and women, not ideologues or "leaders" (read tyrants, gang bosses). Great men and women who influenced generations of people to regard one another as brothers, who had the good will to challenge their contemporaries to make the world work for everybody, with no one left out. Example? Oh, from our time, say, Albert Einstein. Carl Sandburg. Mohandas Gandhi. Jane Addams. Frank Lloyd Wright. From centuries past, say, Thomas Jefferson. Abraham Lincoln. Ralph Waldo Emerson. Walt Whitman. Emily Dickinson. (Strange. Each of my examples would probably be considered of the left in today's chatter of alignments. Well, it can't be helped.) Of more recent times, there are Vaclav Havel, Nelson Mandela, Mikhail Gorbachev and Martin Luther King, among others. There. I have said what I wanted to say. I think civilization has a chance. (I hesitate to fix the odds.) Because of our terrible and wondrous creative power, each of us has a place in the choir, whether or not we are willing to sing.

And there is this. Whenever two or more of us gather as we did the other night at your home, and we laugh together and stretch toward the truth, and enjoy the moment and the food, just what do you think that does to the direction of motion at the peak of the bell curve? Well? Well? Talk about power!

As I said to you the other night, I think there is reason to be optimistic because there are people like you scattered throughout the world who can consciously choose to align (No, not "organize"!), align silently and add to the probability of a civilized humanity by being the decent human beings that you are. That, for starters, any of us can do.

III

Thoughts and Mutterings

The Year Begins: January 1, 1994

The year begins. A door opens. Light pours in. Yes, there is form. Shapes shimmer and dance among the infinite spaces of light and thoughts. Thoughts. Deepak Chopra calls them impulses of energy/information. We find ourselves in an expanding universe of these, ours to generate, to give form to, and echo among ourselves in real tears and real laughter, dancing, music, loving, propagating. We are now privileged to let go of the cloned thoughts, which iterate and reiterate to form the illusions of solidity called the past. The actual past does not need to be recreated and we are reluctant to believe that. We are reluctant because we think that by letting go we will lose the joy and good times which we would hold on to.

Lost cause. They cannot be held onto. Not because they are not real, for they are real, but because joy and good times exist only now. The fact is that if you would have joy and good times and the light glimmering in your life, it can only be now. If you would have the past, then you will live among the frozen forms, the joyless facsimiles of what once was.

Yet you do not lose the past by letting it go to find its place in time. At any given moment you can call up the recorded segment of any moment of the history of the universe. The frontiersmen of science tell us that we contain the library of the universe in every cell and thought. But look. Given the choice to re-experience a facsimile of some moment from the past, or to create from the quantum universe of energy and thought anything that one desired, why would one choose the past?

But we do. We do choose the past. We choose to bring up the facsimiles of the past, alter them ever so slightly, thus giving them the illusion of dimension and legitimacy in time, thus ignoring the fact that by so doing we are also legitimizing that of the past which we would never want to experience again but must, now, in facsimile. Must, I say? Yes, once chosen. These facsimiles can be regretted, delighted in, or denied, but only if they have first been chosen and attended to.

Denial, then, is the act of covering with a cover of black blankness, opaque nothingness, solid as a black hole in deepest space, the facsimiles which we have made real and solid at great apparent cost of creative energy.

Here, now, we can begin. Here, now, we can step out of the sculpture gardens of our past, shapes beloved in their beauty and shapes cloaked, denied, titillating, to be struggled against, or wallowed in. Or, we can choose to create whatever pleases us. The choice is to invest our attention into being alive, or to rattle around among the forms which seem to be alive but are not; the facsimiles of times past.

What I have been saying here I intend as a challenge, as a declaration of thought to be tested in the course of living our lives. I claim no authority to say these things, but I say you and I have the opportunity to choose to attend to them or not, as they form in the conversations of our life and time. For now, there are conversations coming forth from scientists exploring the edges of the universe where the perceivable gives way to the ephemeral, which seem to be telling us what the sage Vasishtha said so long ago, "Infinite worlds appear and disappear in the vast expanse of my own consciousness, like motes of dust dancing in a beam of light."

Ancient wisdom, quantum physics, thee and me free of the past, empowered and creative; that's where we all are, now.

Faces

I knock for a time loudly on the door before it opens and the face I had dreamed looks at me puzzled. Puzzlement and recognition flash on and off, that face a coastal lighthouse showing the way. We continue to look at one another in the place where time loses its power to mold and shape what seems to be. One of us must speak or we will both disappear. The face speaks then, "Yes?" To which I reply, "Yes."

One of us now speaks and then the other and from the speaking there arises a great longing to be one and then the other. And the longing speaks not of emptiness or things missing; it speaks of the fullness of this moment here, this space now, this wholeness become what it always was, each minute particle of which is whole and all and no thing ever, and more.

This face, a universe. This face an immense music come to be in chords outflowing into galaxies, becoming themselves, beyond and beyond. This face, all faces, gather now in yes. I say yes and there is now loud knocking on the doors, oh yes, on every door.

"Come," I say, "come take my hand."

We walk now around the lake and upward through the wood trail soft padded by the leaves of fall now soggy from the melt of spring. We stop and look upon the faces we have brought with us, picnic baskets of all we have been and are and are to be. Looking out each to each puzzled and aware how little we know of who we are, yet how familiar we are! Familiar as is the Earth now spinning and spinning utterly, utterly still.

Smiles echo, reverberate, replicate, spin off surrounding each and all of us, bring laughter now and we dance hand in hand to drum beat from the center of us, from the spinning Earth so still. Smiles extending out and out, drum beat centering and enclosing all and one. One laugh. One smile. One face. One silence spinning, spinning still.

Christmas 1991

Every year is different and very much the same. Whatever changed during this past year has changed before for one or another of us. Births, weddings, deaths and moves. Graduations. Promotions. Divorces. Wins. Losses. Old stories.

It occurs to me this year to ask of the year's adventure, "Did all of life get brighter? Or dimmer?" Asking that, I immediately see that I have a choice. Did all of life get brighter during this past year? I chose yes. But then, I have chosen yes far more often than not. Life does get brighter when I choose it so. "Brighter?" you say. Yes, brighter, as in what happens after the dawn. Brighter. No, not necessarily smarter. Brighter in a perception sense. We see more when it's brighter. What's that? Old eyes, you say, see things dimmer. That's not the brightness I'm talking about. I'm talking about the light in things, through and from and of things. Brighter, I say, like the chandelier dims and brightens by our choice at the switch. Like, I say, but different in that the light I am speaking of is more. I mean it flows on and on. Always. We choose whether or not we experience it as brighter or dimmer.

So blessing is brighter. Laughter is brighter. Thoughts of beloved friends. Yes you, beloved, forever friend. Children and grandchildren. Nephews and nieces. Cousins. Those here already and those yet to be, and yes, those of you who have entered, acted and already left this present stage. Brighter. Getting home out of the storm. Brighter. Choices, all. Thoughts, all. Brighter, we say.

So, gyre ye with us, on out of this year......and into next year......Brighter!

Miracles

Yesterday's activities were accompanied by a sense of happenings out beyond the edges of my attention. Yes I was here doing my work, driving, conversing, reading, all in pattern as expected, plus an increasing rhythm of.......what?

I have a sense of major shifts of focus going on in the world conversation. If I were given to playing seer or prophet I could say of this sense such words as, portent, omen; I could declare a perception of shapes, of revealed guilts and dark retributions even tribulations to come. I could choose that they be ego things with fear, anger and catastrophe in them. Or, I could choose that this sense is but the early glitterings of miracles coming, due at last from our pregnant praying; mind seeds blowing in the wind; landing; sprouting. So, presumptuously, I made a choice and I offer it for your consideration.

I chose miracles and there was brightening and laughter, poems and songs like ripening fruit waiting out there where our world is soon to be. I chose miracles for human being. Presumptuously. And, why not? I declared no one was to be left out. Actually I declare that now, and now expands to fill the spaces called yesterday and tomorrow; concentric, expanding rings of now. Miracles expanding.

Listen. I heard that. "Now expands to fill and modify the spaces we call yesterday and tomorrow. Concentric expanding spheres of now; miracles expanding."

Now=being=zero in relation to the ego's world; the conversations of that world. Now=zero in relation to matter, energy, space and time; zero in relation to Homo-sapiens, and all Zero's creatures great and small. Now=silence. Now=our silent center, our being. By choosing miracles my choice is now. By choosing to be now my choice is miracles.

I think of artists and performers. I think of divers, gymnasts, dancers, skaters—all action of excellence in the world of matter, energy, space and time. I think of the possibilities of human being in this jewel of a planet. And again I think of how now expands to occupy the past, the future and the present, on the verge, the very edges of time. And then, there is practice.

Practice, in which excellent performance and the expression of beauty shows up, is practice which takes place right here, on the verge, the edges of time. Such practice is the doorway, or bridge, through or across which the miracle of now is accessed. The creator, the performer and the appreciator dance here together—now—as miracle.

The common denominator of creator, performer and appreciator is practice; the choice made and made again in the present on the verge of now, the very edges of time.

To strive for, to yearn for, to hope for miracles in the absence of practice in the present, on the edges of now, is to believe in and be open to magic.

Magic is the illusion of being the effect of, or the agent of, some external force or power. Magic is the delusion that human being is other-controlled.

Miracles are in the self-chosen participation of human being, now, practicing possibilities which show up on the verge, on the edges of time.

Michelangelo daily chipped away on the marble, doing at each present moment a one-of-a-kind motion with results which accumulated as chips of marble in time and on the floor. And from this practice emerged, showed up, this forever thing, this now of a marbled miracle which evokes human being; not chips piling on the floor of time; human being, the miracle constantly happening.

I think of Bach, of Isaac Stern, of friendships, of mothers and fathers, of sisters and brothers. I think again of skaters and quarterbacks and poets and all the daily practitioners who let the chips fall away in time; who learn to expect at least aliveness and sometimes excellence in each moment of practice and are willing for the surprise of miracles to emerge, to become what is so.

Accomplished practitioners are often heard to say that excellence results from 10% inspiration and 90% perspiration, meaning work, meaning practice. And what is not as often said is that it is from practice that inspiration comes forth and expands from now to fill the spaces called yesterday and tomorrow; concentric, expanding rings of now. Miracles expanding.

From practice comes inspiration. From inspiration comes idea. From inspired idea comes value, the practiced form emerging. Thus there is art, now, expanding, to occupy the past, the future and the present, on the verge, the very edges of time.

What's Happening

Much has been written about this time. It has been referred to as the end time. The end of the world. Armageddon. The Apocalypse. We are definitely beset by an onslaught of terrorism, wars, rumors of wars, earthquakes, volcanoes, starvation, breakdown of civilization, etc. Large numbers of our fellow human beings are fixated upon images of these dire happenings as though they are inevitable and soon to be realized.

In our silent conversations we have touched upon the possibility of an alternative, in which the end of the world could be experienced as a transformation of consciousness whereby it gradually becomes apparent that the dire happenings are being called forth because we humans with our power to co-create are fixated on them. The end of the world that comes forth from fear is just that, a product of our power to co-create from fear.

I propose that the end of the world is the end of the world as we made it from our fear, our egotism, our unwillingness to choose love instead of fear as our motivating reason to be. I propose that we have a choice in the matter. We can choose love in the place of fear. Our choice for love would most certainly bring about a dramatic end of the world as we now suffer it. What would be left? Why, a perfectly lovely small planet peopled with Humanity, we, sibling children of the Creator.

So, we are postulating that it is not necessary for the world to end in fear-based chaos. It could end, this world as we now know it and suffer it; it could end miraculously. Perhaps both? There is the idea of the rapture, of God taking up "His" people and letting the rest of humanity perish in their misery.

The problem with that is that we are all His creations, and we are as we were created from the beginning, saint and Joe Normal alike. God's creations were, are now and are forever. No. Not both. Not some of us sunk into permanent misery and others lifted up by some outside magic and carried away. We are experiencing much that Revelations has declared. We are also experiencing an increase of light and sanity amid the apocalyptic events upon which we habitually, even addictively, focus. This light is available to all, not a select few. We are living in times of crisis following crisis out there in the world. And we are living in times when, one by one by one, Humanity is opening to the presence of this light, and from and into those openings pours the light. Not magic. Not some outside force from on high. This light is the light that enlivens us and bubbles forth from deep within each of us and is sustained by our use of it unto infinity. It is ours to use. It is our authentic power. Thus the old world is transformable. We humans have the capability to live together on this planet, motivated, as Gary Zukav says, by harmony, cooperation, sharing and reverence for life. Really!

So why not?

Desire

There is a little black book titled *The Impersonal Life*. It was written by Joseph S. Benner, who defined the work as a God-given "process." About fifteen years ago the book came to my attention and, in the reading and my attempts to "get" it, there began a process which included completing and subsequently re-reading A Course in Miracles, and then again, a rereading of the little black book.

The Course and the black book are the pure quill. They stir in me the sense, the realization that there is a Spiritual Reality of which I and each of us is a part. I would now add the following titles of books which, like *The Impersonal Life*, also served to nudge me along: *The Seat of the Soul* by Gary Zukav; the six volumes (to date) of *Conversations With God* by Neale Donald Walsch. Any and all of the books by Deepak Chopra, especially, *How to Know God*. And recently, new to me, a series of books from the Greater Community Way of Knowledge by Marshall Vian Summers, which offers a 365-day study course of powerful guidance in the ways of wisdom. Also another delight of a book, *Excuse Me, Your Life is Waiting*, by Lynn Grabhorn.

This morning my focus is on desire. Desire is a God-given attribute of human being. As I interpret the above mentors, desire, my desire, focuses and channels and is itself the creative power from the Center, from Creation, from God. Free will is another attribute from God, by which I can focus and channel universal creative power toward what I want and desire, no matter what it is. If it is ego driven, then what I focus on will take form and will be mine to experience.

Often I have desired some thing or goal, focused on it and attained it, this, often enough to testify that there is this creative power that manifests as desire. Desire causes what is focused upon to take form. And then comes that emptiness, the sense that, surely, there must be more! This is followed by the plaintive "Is that all there is?!" Often in this bleak place, if allowed and listened for, there will come a deeper yearning followed by a glimmer of response, not from "out there" but from a deeper inner place, a desire which is more than "I want." It calls out,

"Ah, I would be...." This is well expressed in this quote from *Conversations With God*, wherein I yearn to "recreate myself anew in the grandest version of the greatest vision I ever held about Who I Am." I would call that a True Desire.

I seek now to know in the course of living life itself the difference between my personal free-will desires, things and realities associated with ego survival here on Earth, and that Desire which transcends those things and leads to the awareness of the Sacred within. I would have to say that desire and Desire both occur with God's blessing and empowerment, in order that they be learning experiences for me. Therefore it is better to follow my desire even when it is not clear what is ego desire and what is True Desire.

We are told in the above sources that anyone can learn to open a clearing, a Stillness within—that there is a Center, a Silence in each of us, a sort of inner chapel, to which we can retire, and there cause the Stillness that brings forth the power of Creation, of God.

In that stillness, now, I will center. I am in my sacred place.

Now some practice in Desire. I desire:

1. A healthy and functioning body. Clear eyesight. Clear hearing. Dump this 80-year-old one? No. Not until completion. Health, strength and vitality enough for enjoyment of this body until completion. Completion? Yes. I came here with a work to do. It is not complete. I would let go the concern about my physical condition. I thus shut down the worry machine and replace it with the light. I stand steady in the light. I say "Yes!" to harmony, cooperation, sharing and reverence for life.

2. What now is my work to do? How, where to be about the Father's business? What is here in my silent center? Learn and share. Be that which you have been given. Be it, do it and accept what comes; ample supply, always flowing through. Not as in wealthy, but as in whatever is needed, and even more. I acknowledge this as God-given and I declare my gratefulness. I hereby shut down the worry machine having to do with supply and replace it with the light. I stand steady in the light. I say "Yes!" to harmony, cooperation, sharing and reverence for life.

3. Several years ago I decided to use early morning space and time to "edge along my frontier" by seeking the silence in reading, contemplation, meditation and by writings such as these mutterings. The desire implicit in doing this is to be a center of light which would invite the light of others to come

forth. And, wouldn't you know it? The ego wanted to get into the act. Oh yes! The ego, little 'i,' wants recognition. It wants to be admired, praised. It wants to be seen. It is not interested in bringing forth the light from others, in fact, just the opposite. The light from others is competition to the ego. How little the poor thing knows about the creative power of alignment! So I shut down the ego-machine and I stand steady in the light.

4. And now it is so that I am the authority I have been seeking. I am. Impersonally. I am my authority. From within I am, I emanate a light from a central source, a Silent Central Source, forever replenished as it gives forth. So what has become of desire? Now it seems that there is always a place to be. Always a work to do. Always a song to sing. A poem in process. Always, in every moment there is completion and beginning. And there is no end to it. All this results when I stand steady in the light while being the grandest version of the greatest vision I ever held about who I am.

Then?

5. Practice, practice, practice; being steady in the light.

Note: All of the books mentioned above are available from various sources on the Internet.

A Declaration of Autonomy

The next great step for mankind is the result of one giant step by each individual human being. That giant step is the transition of the individual into the possibility of what a human being can be. In making this transition an individual will step forth from a mind set by which he has identified himself with the animal creature which he perceives himself and his body to be. In this mind set humanity has, in the main, made use of his creative power, sometimes appropriately as explorer and manipulator of the physical universe, and more often inappropriately as he is thrown to the use of his creative power as force for the persuasion and control of his fellow human beings.

Now we are on a threshold where we can gain access to, and express as beings, the possibility of what a human being can be. This is not to be achieved by persuasion, by an army, by an election nor by revolution, and yet the result can be the transformation of humanity on this planet to all that it can be.

To cross this threshold a declaration of individual autonomy is required. This declaration is made from and in the stand taken by each individual to be himself or herself, to be the possibility it is to be a human being.

As an individual human being I do declare on this date, March 7, 1985, the following:

At those points of my daily life and activity where engagement with another or other human beings takes place, I am responsible to function as a bridge to the possibility of being what it means to be human. To function as that bridge means to, myself, be alive in the possibility of being human. To function as that bridge, I, myself, must identify and let go of the ground of being in which I and nearly all of us find ourselves; and then to construct from abstract values a new ground of being; a paradigm which is the possibility of what one man/mankind can be. To be that bridge means to be committed to an ongoing conversation with those with whom I am responsible to engage. And this I promise to do.

A Declaration of Autonomy

To do this means that I will listen to the listening of those with whom I engage, to the end that the possibility of being human is a growing reality; becomes an existing and evident structure within which I and others engage in our dance. It means that my conversations will not include argument nor rudeness, will not include confessions nor accusations. It means I will make commitments. It means I will be my word. It means I will say what I will do and will actually do what I say. I will use as a referent this stand I now take. I now build on that referent a ground of being, a base of experience in the practice of these conversations: these committed conversations.

I shall know I am doing this because I say so, by declaration, and by the increasing energy that is available to me; by moments of joy, whether or not my action is perceived or the results are recognized.

Eve of War — September 1990

Here are some mutterings about the trouble in the sandlot not so far away from here. On this day we are confronting another war. What follows applies to Desert Storm, Yugoslavia and Israel/Palestine. It took me a week or more to bring my reactions under control and consciously let the fear and anger go. This has to do with mind and consciousness, not foreign policy.

As human beings we have the power to create the world of our experience. We have the power to create fear-generated misery, ugliness and savagery for ourselves and our families and our environment, which includes all other people; and our mental, emotional and physical universes. We have that awesome power and we also have the power to create a love-generated world of plenty, magnificence, beauty and joy for all. Quite simply, our environment is formed by who and how we are in thought and the subsequent use of the creative power of our thought.

War is the exercise of human creative power to control the behavior of designated enemies by violent means. An enemy is whatever the combatant declares enemy to be. Every warlike move by any combatant nation is declared by all sides to be defensive. "They started it" is the flag all sides fly on the road to war.

To invade another country is to use direct violence against the people of a sovereign state. This has long been considered unacceptable behavior of one nation in relation to another; except, that is, in recent decades when invasion of another country is declared necessary in defense of the invaders' national honor. Or, say, their sovereign rights.

So of course it becomes justifiable to proclaim that it is the obligation of a people, as it is an individual, to prevent violent harm to self, family, tribe and nation. The result then is another war, neatly justified and tragic in its shaping of the future. Forgotten yet again is the fact that prevention of violence by violent means only causes future violence. An American president once stated that we would have peace even if it meant going to war for it. It was he who ordered the atomic bombing of two cities in Japan. Most Americans agreed that this saved

Eve of War—September 1990

many lives. Personally I have always had difficulty differentiating between "our" lives and "their" lives. I clearly remember the gut wrenching impact when I first learned that the bomb had been dropped on Hiroshima and Nagasaki without warning.

The fact is, that those who think, dream and attend to violence in their thought inevitably speak and listen to violent words, and inevitably experience violence on their person, family, and others who buy into that fear and anger-generated violence. Inevitably! Sound familiar? It should. Try this: "He who lives by the sword shall die by the sword." I am told that some form of this statement is written in most if not all of the holy scriptures of the world. And a corollary to that is that anyone, or any nation, who is experiencing invasion or other violence, has thought, dreamed, spoken and listened to words of violence, born from his choice of mindset, of fear. At the very least they have failed to counter, with sanity and peacefulness, the popular mindset of fear and prejudice and general ill will toward all alien others, ethnic or religious or political.

Violence, as it is with any activity, begins with thought, takes first form with words, and manifests in action. Violent and hateful thought can be changed. Those who fear others and therefore hate and desire the destruction of others can learn to change their inner and outer conversations, their habits of mind.

To change thought from violence is as simple as it is difficult. In fact it is difficult only because it is unbelievably simple. Violent thought occurs when the thinker has chosen (yes chosen!) fear as the mind-set and motivator of his thinking. When the choice is made for fear, then all of the perceptors of the chooser, in fact all of his creative power, mobilizes to gather evidence to establish the legitimacy of that fear. When from this creative process that which is feared becomes real, then the creative power generates the means for the destruction of that which is feared. This then causes accelerating cycles of violence and invasions and war. Always caused by them, over there. Or rather, always caused by our fear of them, over there.

I propose that there is a better way to go about living our lives and sharing this really bountiful planet. Instead of our habitual stance of fear, we could take another stance. We could look at our planet and the physical universe and the animal life and the plant life and the seas and the fishes of the seas, and acknowledge that we have at hand a bountiful table set here in the wilderness of space. We are a people, Humanity, on this lovely small planet. We can recognize that whatever happens to one of us here on this planet, happens to all of us. We could acknowledge that we are connected, each of us, to all of us, and, although we are connected and are as one, we are each a unique and sparkling individual, like unto no other one of us in the universe.

I therefore choose to declare as my stance in life, that I am here with all other humans in order to make the world work for the benefit of everyone on the planet, with no one left out.

Now I happen to know that there are many, many people present in every city, village and hamlet in the world, who have been operating from the stance that the use of violence on fellow humans or on the environment is no longer an option. Fear has been let go in favor of love. Because so many have taken that stance, some remarkable changes have taken place in the world in the past several years. Willis Harmon called it a global mind change. Others have called it a paradigm shift in consciousness. I like to think of it as a change in the focus and quality of our inner and outer conversation. Others consider it divine intervention. Whatever it is called, this shift of consciousness has created a context of possiblity in which human creative power has been operating with remarkable results; results that politics and war and other fear-generated exercises have nowhere near matched in thousands of years of human history. We can actually see and feel the possibility of a world in which war is really unthinkable, in which the choice of fear is seen as an aberration and not normal human behavior.

We need to say, all of us, "I and my nation are addicted to violence and war—to the use of our God-given creative power as force, against the creative power as force of my neighbors and their nations. This addiction is depriving the human race of the marvelous possibilities with which we have been endowed as human being."

This must come from the heart, with true humility, and calls for the strength of faith that comes from letting go of fear and letting the God-given creative power do its miracle work.

Each of us can say, right now, "I choose love and good will toward my fellow human beings, rather than succumb again to my addiction to violence and to war."

Then we need to remind each other and support each other in continuing to choose and co-create, as Werner Erhart said, a world that works for everyone with no one left out.

It is now August of 2003.

Violence still reigns in its many brutalizing forms. The monstrous power centers of the Cold War have disengaged, but only after having deposited deadly

Eve of War — September 1990

caches of automatic weapons, ammunition and explosives of every sort on every continent. Both sides have left, neglected, huge stockpiles of chemical and biological weapons deteriorating into God knows what catastrophes to be. There are rusting atomic submarines ready to contaminate the oceans of the world.

Another form of violence is now center stage, whereby small cadres of humans can cause destrucion and mayhem that were once only within the power of mighty nations. Now we know it is possible for two men, armed with rifles and hand guns only, to randomly murder one citizen after another and tie up the emergency and police forces of a region for days.

As always, violence only begets itself. Even that sick logic breaks down when suicide bombers are considered. Those slow to learn are trying to come up with ways to use their monstrous fire power to eradicate tiny clusters of terrorists. Homes, buildings, highways and bridges are now vulnerable to these terrorists. They now can equal the carnage that has reduced cities and their infrastructures into rubble. This only brings forth more terrorists. Unlike rats who learn that certain behaviors are rewarded and others are fruitless, the war chiefs of our time keep doing more of the same old thing.

More than ever, the transformation spoken of above makes sense. The crisis in our world is not economic or political or military, it is spiritual. It has to do with what we believe about ourselves and each other. Fortunately, it is possible to change one's beliefs, especially those that are not working. The means and methods necessary to transform our world into sanity are at hand and people by the millions are making use of them.

These means and methods are varied. It has always been possible for a sincere person to call out to the Universe, "What am I here for?" or some such earnest plea. The world's literature attests to the fact that many quite sane and wise men and women feel that such pleas are answered, that it is even possible to have a two-way conversation with that Universe in whatever form seems workable to the supplicant. There are many forms that this conversation can take, but it has become increasingly clear that the communication lines are open and clear for anyone willing to engage. Those who have had the courage to enter into such conversation are doing what I have come to call "The Work". The Work is always personal; one being to the One Universe. The communication lines are from the Center Being of the Universe to the Center within the individual, and return. It is two way, intuitive, and mostly silent. There is no outer Authority involved in doing The Work. This is not to say that this is the only way that one can experience transformation. I can assume the authority to say, for me, it seems to be a way that works; unless and until there are changes. Then it is my responsibility to include the changes in consciousness in order for The Work to continue authentically.

This transformation has been taking place among significant numbers of people in increments of one plus one plus one. As these individuals evolved, their transformed presence attracted others in precious ones and couples and their children. This is world-wide in scope, despite the mayhem so stridently reported on CNN. This incremental transformation has begun to manifest in the form of organizations which reflect the transformation that is spreading rapidly, though it is largely unnoticed by much of humanity. There are thousands of such groups and organizations. Transformation is now being given organizational form by individuals who have taken the consciousness derived from their doing The Work and given it form in the world. As a result these organizations are inclusive rather than exclusive. Neale Donald Walsch of Humanity's Team says, "Ours is not the only way. Ours is but another way." They do not divide the world into things that are good and things that are not good. Instead they focus their energies to discover what is workable in relation to problems they have chosen to address. The test of any idea, method or technique is its workability in relation to the goals and purposes, the mission of the group. Groups of transformed people are open. They say, "Let's try it and see." The following organizations are listed because all are the creations of individuls who have been doing The Work in one form or another, in religious contexts or not. There must be thousands of others; I am sure that they have much in common. These can be found on the Internet.

Humanity's Team
Habitat For Humanity
Doctors Without Borders
Books For Africa
Haiti Outreach

Cause, Change, Create, Transform and Let Be

The following was written in the period just prior to and after the Gulf War I.

Back in 1991, as the Gulf War got underway and the scene in Eastern Europe began to turn ugly, I did what I have learned to do instead of fight, roar and cry: I turned to my word processor and I muttered. I sought to hold to the reality that I/we, imperfect yet perfectable Humanity are at the cause of all this, as follows:

Present on my mental desktop this morning is the juxtaposition of five verbs: to cause, to change, to create, to transform and to let be. Each of us and all of us participate in ongoing conversations, silent as well as out loud. These light up, as though on a TV screen, images and ideas and action which, when energized by our attention, take place in actuality. Our participation in this process is the way by which we cause whatever it is that we experience in living our lives. By attending to the conversation and attending to the images thus projected, we give form to the world we perceive and experience. So, "to cause" is the verb, the word form which is the symbol for our power to cause effects in the world.

For example, a significant percentage of the population of this world is presently experiencing a war somewhere on this planet and this has been so in every decade of the twentieth century. Probably the only 100% agreement that exists among the participants in these conflicts is that someone else is at cause in the matter. All agree that the cause of the conflict lies with the other party or parties. There is a hierarchy of participation that includes the warriors themselves and their families. It includes civilians who live in the place where the bombs are being dropped and other places where terrorist acts are promulgated. It includes the governments who have all chosen the roles they are playing in the conflict. Governments, of course, are individual people playing roles in the context of which they bring focus upon certain levels of conversation, the very conversation which I say causes the experience we are having. To put it succinctly, the wars we experience are caused by our individual participation in conversations which lead to war.

When an Ayatollah, in whatever totalitarian form, calls a nation of people as Khomeini calls the United States, "the Great Satan," this label is taken up and replicated among the population who are the followers of that leader and is then emotionally enhanced, made "real" by demonstrations and chanting. The result, as we all experienced here in 1980, was that we Americans became demons and Satan itself to the Iranian masses. We, in turn, witnessing via TV what we were called, reacted and created a counter conversation that resulted in a demonization of the Ayatollah and his followers. This process is automatic and reactive. It is as though the ravings and chanting of masses of people, the sneering put-downs by presidents, and the hatefulness thus generated were actual physical threats to ourselves and our children and our survival into the future. At this level the process is comparable to the "She hit me first/I did not/You did too" conversations endemic in school yards at recess and in the back seats of family station wagons. As such it is relatively harmless in its sound and fury.

However, if this process continues it begins to form a mind set in which it is possible to consider and justify the destruction of "them, over there." Now add the conscious, calculated, profitable participation in the conversation of munitions makers and high-tech hardware producers. Add further the war mock-ups of the people of the military. Now stir in the sneering put-downs of our politicians toward theirs, draw lines in the sand, and you have most of the essential components that lead up to actual war. Within these conversations we construct the ideologies and the "rationale" for playing war. Now the spark is all that is needed. Pearl Harbor. The invasion from the North of South Korea, the fabricated Gulf of Tonkin incident. The invasion of the autocracy of Kuwait, and, boom! Oh how the hardware flies, killing and maiming and proving what we have been saying all along about "them" over there.

War is caused by our participation in the conversations of war. I am saying our conversations are at cause in the matter. I am saying we, each of us, is at cause. Decades of conversations within the focus of munitions makers, high-tech hardware producers and people of the military and political power centers have produced the means to carry out any war. Government leaders then have the obligation to construct the ideology, the rationale for playing war, and curses and brickbats to any who counsel peaceful solutions.

To cause, then, is to live and breathe and have our being as human being. All that we are experiencing in the world is the result of our power to cause; yes, even the experiences we call Saddam Hussein and George Bush. They reflect, they are the projections of, our ongoing conversations.

Because of this power to cause, we also have the power to change the conditions in which we live. We can change our experience by simply taking our focus off of the conversation which we are currently "screening" and shifting our focus to any other ongoing conversation which we choose. To choose the venue in which each of us places our attention is the process whereby we generate change in our lives. As it is when we click the TV remote control from, say, Channel 4 to Channel 2, we change what we are attending to. But in reality we are still sitting in our chairs and watching TV.

Most individuals go through changes in the course of living their lives. Most of these find that the changes that result from simply shifting from one conversation to another do not seem to bring about betterment, or progress or growth. It takes some thought and insight and self-honesty for any of us to acknowledge that such change is not in itself anything special. We find we are the same person even if we have a new car, or if our team wins "it all," or if we "fall" into or out of "love" or divorce or marry, or lose or gain weight. What we can learn from change is that the power to change is a function of the power to cause.

At some point along the way of personal growth and doing what I call "The Work," we find that we possess a deeper more profound power; the power to create. To cause, to change and to create are gradient functions of our God-given creative power. Because of this creative power, our participation in conversations has the power to cause and the power to change what we are viewing and experiencing. As we become aware of this creative power to cause and to change, the opportunity to shift into another echelon of use of this power begins to show up. Often this shift is the result of asking questions, perhaps like these that follow:

> If I have indeed caused the experience I am living by my participation in the conversations going on around me, then, what if I use my creative power to generate my contribution to the conversation from a base of what do I really, really want, desire, aspire to?
>
> Having been reacting to and responding pro and con to the conversation going on in this time, just as I have in the past, I have found that the stances of both pro and con add to, energize and make real the ongoing realities in my life. Could it be possible to let those conversations go and come up with a conversation entirely other than those? Could there be conversations devoid of pro and con?

Could I bring about in the world more than just change—even a real transformation? Could I do this by generating my conversation from what I would cause if I knew I had the choice and power? Is it true that, in the aggregate, I/we do have that power?

These questions, or others similar, come about naturally as soon as we begin to be aware of the fact of our participation in the conversations which give power and shape, reality actually, to the world we live in.

Implied in that third question is the possibility that, more than just changing things, we could co-create something entirely other in our experience of the world. For example, we could declare it desirable to cause a world that works for everyone with no one left out. That would require a change of our internal and outer conversations of such magnitude as to be a transformation. Consider the caterpillar inching along a twig or leaf. Contemplate the process whereby it changes from larva to pupa. That is change indeed. But it is a change of degree, of a creature slow to move and limited in arena of operation. And then the butterfly! That is transformation. From ovum and sperm to conception to zygote to fetus to embryo, these are changes. Then with the first breath and the living presence of infant, comes transformation.

Perhaps one could insist that change is a gradient of transformation, but it is a gradient in the context of which transformation does not yet occur. Could it be said that the passage of time is involved with change, whereas transformation occurs out of time?

Change is the product of the hard wiring of an organism and transformation is of the being, of the spirit. Change is locked onto a constant relationship to the passage of time. Transformation comes forth from mind, from intention born of profound desire, and it emerges in time at the declaration of the intender. Could this idea contain the seed, the transformation of which would bring to peace the heated controversy about abortion and choice? Transformation takes place in time but brings with it the primal power which is forever timeless. The psychologist Rollo May has said that the point of creative power is now. The same energy is involved but the energy that transforms comes directly from power. The process that only changes comes from, sort of spills out of, what was before, repeating itself on and on, only slightly different in form, hardly different enough to notice.

There is another function which dances with this creative power with which we humans are endowed. This function is the power and ability to let, or let be. It sounds passive. It is not passive. To let be is to practice the tough virtues of patience, of tolerance, of forbearance. To let what is, be as it is, relates to the recognition that there are others in the world learning of their power to cause, to change, to create and transform. To let others go through their own process is a profound acknowledgement of their power to grow.

Control comes into this. We are learning of our own power to create our environment in the images of our choice. We learn to do this by choosing to initiate, to continue, to change and to cease the process of energizing whatever we focus our attention upon. These are functions of our power to control. There is nothing wrong with control—control of our own creative power. Extending that control to others can be interference in their universes, in their right to learn and to grow. Perhaps it would make it clearer to say that control is good when applied to the direction of one's own energy and focus, and control is often interference when applied to the energy and focus of another or others' energy. Control can be empowerment when one's energy and focus are aligned with the energy and focus of another or others.

How much mischief we get into when we misuse our creative power for the control of others! Couple that error (which is all but universal) with our addiction to the use of our creative power as force directed toward control of others, and we have gotten a handle on the history of human inhumanity to human; from Og, the caveman, to George Bush and Saddam Hussein. And to each of us as we struggle to come to peaceful terms with our awesome creative power.

And it is a struggle to let it be emotionally as missiles drop in Israel, and bombs and rockets tear up the lives of Iraqis, and some mad scheme brings millions of gallons of oil to spoil the waters of the Persian Gulf for perhaps generations to come, and nearly one million soldier brothers poise to annihilate one another from the face of the Earth. Add to that the shriveling of the brave possibilities that were blooming just months ago in Eastern Europe. And to that add the pent-up aching ethnic turmoil bubbling forth in old spots and new. It is such a temptation to look to Saddam and to George and to Mikhail and to others of the old world order, and accuse them, "Look, look what you have done to these marvelous days of hope." And yet, calm in the Center there is a voiceless message that says to me, "Let it be. Hold, hold steady in the light. There is work yet to do, and every one of you is needed so that what must be can be worked out. This is not the end of things. This is winter and there will be spring. You are needed for the planting, so let it be."

Desert Storm — The Aftermath, 1992

My excuse for harping on the disaster in the Gulf is that it has dominated my mind and consciousness to the exclusion of sane, creative and benign considerations which go along with with peace and goodwill to all Humankind. I want to say this final statement about "operation smart barbarism" (final, unless some other idiocy comes up, such as rearming everybody).[1] You know, just one more for the road.

So "victory is ours!" Kuwait is "free." Casualties are amazingly "light." It took seven months of "coalition presence" in the desert, six weeks of air attack and 100 hours of ground war to achieve the utter devastation of the Iraqi armed forces. Speaking of casualties in human body terms, consider tens of thousands of Iraqi and Kuwaiti casualties; and probably more. And say nothing of the tortured and the torturers and the emotionally devastated soldiers and citizens and the new crop of set-upon and brutalized Palestinians in Kuwait, and elsewhere. To say nothing of the enturbulation which I have allowed in to me, and my "world." Consider the bombed out homes and the terrorized mothers and children and the husbandless and fatherless families; then speak with "pride" about victory and casualties that are "light." Consider the impact of generations more of resentment and hatred that is taking form amid the months to come of smoke and oily rain. Consider, oh God, the helpless oil-sogged cormorant slowly sinking in the ooze. Crude oil, crude man! Indeed!

So what do I know from all of this? George Bush has nearly 90% approval rating, according to the polls. At the onset of this debacle there was a significant minority who opposed our military intervention in the Gulf. Now there is a very small scattering of 10% or less who view the whole exercise not as the birth of a New World Order, but as a progenitor of a new barbarism. I take my stand. I connect with that scattering. Is that fair? New barbarism? Certainly we accept

---

1. [It did.]

that the Iraqi invaders of Kuwait behaved as barbarians. I am saying the coalition's reaction has expanded that barbarism to include the degradation of the ecosystems of the region and enough turmoil and resentment and hatred to "justify" further the barbarism and counter barbarism which we call war, and for generations to come. A barbarism, sad to say, which is endorsed by the doctrine of an eye for an eye and a tooth for a tooth. A doctrine which lies like a coiled snake in the the "holy" scriptures of most of mankind.

And yes, I am glad that Saddam Hussein has been rendered powerless in the world, if only temporarily. Now if kindness and tolerance and reason and, above all, forgiveness can find rootholds among the wheat and tares of our human consciousness and sprout and grow among us, perhaps nourishment for the spirit can find its way to the core of us despite the devastation. Yes. So, to that end, what can I do?

First, I declare that whenever we as a nation or a coalition of nations engage in war, we have the duty and the responsibility to acknowledge that our prewar policies have failed. Whenever, in fact, we are at war, we must acknowledge that our connection, our communication with others has failed. We can crow all we want as winners and blame and finger point as losers. But this fact remains and must be confronted before any real healing can occur: we created a war by failing to use our minds and our virtues and our love and God-given creativeness. Up to now all nations participating in war blame the other side for the war. This is patently an avoidance and a denial of the fact that all parties were responsible for their parts in the conflicts that finally became a war.

I hereby acknowledge that, as a citizen of these United States I am responsible for the form and the direction of my government. I am responsible for the character and quality of the leadership of my nation. No, this is not grandiosity. "I" includes all human being. In that context then the character of our leadership is a reflection of our aggregate character and consciousness, to which I contribute, moment by moment, by my thoughts spoken and muttered silently within myself.

Yes, I know, there is forgiveness. Well, since I have come to know that forgiveness means letting go of the past, I'll do just that. But first, this.

The context in which people of power presently operate, the idea that "our" casualties were light appears to relate not at all to the fact that human and ecological casualties of Desert Storm are huge. There is small regard for the human and environmental degradation that has been caused. The idea that victory means "our" casualties are light and "theirs" are crushing has been the mindset of egoism, of patriotism, for centuries. Those who think "ours" includes all others have been, up to now, a minority. And I am persuaded that this minority is growing and that a new paradigm is all but visible, even now in the clamor and whistles of "victory" of one "side" over the other. This new paradigm is actually the oldest of all, the paradigm in which we are and always have been sibling children of the Creator. Here, we are and always have been, one Humanity. Here our power is our creativity with which we have all been endowed by our Creator. Here we operate as autonomous individuals. Here we do The Work.

It is likely that those operating in the present power paradigm have turned away from doing The Work. Progress in The Work is measured by progress in practicing virtues which would have us give where the opportunity is to take, or to exercise our power from our Humanity rather than from our egoism. The Work? Yes. I say that each human being has The Work to do to accomplish at last the character to be all that he can be. The Work is demanding and soul stirring and one day probably becomes all-encompassing. When one is doing The Work, the identification of self begins to include the consideration that "I" am larger than "me" and "I" includes all others and that we, without exception, are sibling children of one God. The perception begins to form that "I" am a separate being at the level of operating in a body and a personality, and "I" am part of all at the level of Humanity, of Human Being. "I" am all of Humanity, even George Bush, even Saddam Hussein; and other patriots.

As this work is done one moves out of the adversarial paradigm wherein mean, arrogant politics and war and other abuses and misuses of human creative power are acceptable choices. The fact that few in political power have moved beyond the adversarial paradigm attests to the probability that few in positions of power continue to do The Work, the disciplined practice of which brought them to power.

In that context, then, Bush, Baker and Cheney comprise a warhawk cadre who must now be forgiven. I mean, they too, were created by the same Creator who brought forth Mother Teresa. This new *troika*, too, someday, will be called upon, again, to get on with doing The Work.

Yes, it's dawning on me too! Here I am still studying war when, so obviously, I too must get on with doing The Work! Somewhere, in that place where forgiveness is possible I hear the voice of Mahalia Jackson, singing (just listen to that cathedral of a voice!) down there by the riverside......"ain't gonna study war no more!"

Alas. That was written in 1992. In less than a decade the eyes and teeth exchanged again. Warhawks srill ahorse, add Rice, Rumsfeld and Ashcroft.

The Concept of God

God laughed when I sat down at the computer to play. Actually what happened was that I sat here just now, typed in the subject which you see above, rubbed my hands together, stretched my knuckles and......then, I laughed. I am still laughing, quietly, inside, because I am alone here in my writing place. Alone, that is, except for Him and me, laughing.

Now there is a sense of *deja vu*. Years and years ago, shortly after I had passed unscarred through my second stint at being absolutely certain of it all, and had wandered about quite long enough as an "earnest searcher," I put down the fifteenth book I was halfway through, and I said something like this: "Okay, that's enough! I don't want to hear any more words about it. I want the direct experience of what is so and no more words about what is so." There was laughter then also. It wasn't mine.

That was several decades ago as we count time. And it was only a moment ago. In fact it is right now. I have lived through decades since right now and I have met some remarkable people and have had some personal adventures, inner as well as outer. I've done some dumb and hurtful things and have hurt some myself and through it all I have had a sense that what I was experiencing I was causing and that it all added up to what is so. And it also added up to my sitting here, laughing with God, here in my Cosmic-Global-Societal-Worldview MacIntosh room. Okay, I am going to repeat something I have said before. It is what was so for me a couple of years ago. It still is.

>All that God created is, was and will be.
>Each and all of human being is a created being, created by God,
>>and thus is, was and will be.
>Is, was and will be is now. Now is Eternity.

We humans are connected Now,
> All and each of us and God.
Always and Now we are the creation ongoing.

We are endowed with free will which is, at last,
> the opportunity to say "yes" or "no" to what is so.

We experience our "yes" to creation as
> Joy, as Light, as Beauty, as Love out-flowing.

We experience our "no" to creation as
> fear, as hatred, as limitation, as darkness and war.

Our bodies and our names are symbols, as words are symbols.

We have our bodies in order to operate in time.
> The happiness, and the conditions of survival
> of our bodies reflect our "yes" or our "no."

Our connection to one another is as brother and sister beings—
> sibling children of God. We always know that this is so and
> we tend to forget that this is so.

We can, at any moment, say "Yes," and we are connected.
> This is what forgiveness is.

We can, at any moment, say "No," and
> we seem to be separate. And this is forgetfulness.

We always have the choice to forgive now and forever;
> to thus know Joy and Light and Love expanding,
> or to forget and live the forgetful life in time.

Now I know that my saying that God created....etc. does not add much to the "what's so" of anyone else. And I know that I don't know it experientially except during rare milliseconds of clarity. I do know that operating as though it were so is an integrative and unifying process, and those activities which make up the living of my life have tended to work quite well since I began to operate from that assumption. And since my personal life expands outward to include wife, family,

MacIntosh, serendipitous gatherings of others on the path and Society and a Global, Cosmic Worldview…..well, why not?

There is another experiential base upon which I take this stand. It is my observation that people who operate as though they were only physical bodies with names, who assume that there are no realities other than those available to the five senses, often tend to find it justifiable to "terminate" these and other creatures in large numbers. They do this apparently without regret, remorse, or a "thank you, fellow creature." Yes, I know, a lot of this terminating activity derives as well from alignments with and assumptions about angry and punishing Gods, and other ideologies.

Fairness requires me to say, "One of my best friends is an atheist." This good man, a refugee as a child from the Russian Civil War, believes that only perceiving is believing. He is an engineer, a man of high character and impeccable integrity. He simply equates "religious" superstition with the word God and hasn't felt the need to ask further questions. And that's really okay with me. He knows that I come from a different place and that's okay (somewhat condescendingly) with him. And there is a whole universe for us to share and to enjoy as friends.

What I want to make clear is that integrating the thought of God with my life considerations "works" for me. I know that no-God "works" for others. Getting a handle on what is actually so is a process that is deeply personal, also universal, and very likely there is always more to it. I accept it as a blessing that there is also laughter along the way.

Honor the Order of Things

I say that there is an increasing number of individuals in the world who have worked their way to their personal frontiers of mind and consciousness and are pressing outward into new territory, and forming the language of their progress as they go. I propose that every tiny movement made by any one of these toward a clearer perception of what is actually so makes what is so that much more perceivable for the rest of us. This is so, because on our frontiers, we are connected; we are open to one another because we share the intention to extend outward, toward the Light. And, here on our frontiers where the Light enhances our stretching, we are experiencing the possibility of human transformation of a magnitude thought impossible not long ago.

It is possible that each of us is involved in this process at some level of our awareness. The clearer we are, the closer we get to what is so, the brighter the light, the more appropriate and effective the action in the world. Every moment of our being is action. Every word we speak silently, or every word that "proceedeth out of the mouth" becomes the form for the very experience of our lives.

Listen to us! Talk about action! Talk about power! We are manifesting quite literally our conversation in the world. This was true 4,000 years ago and 2,000 years ago and 200 years ago, and forty and thirty and ten, and even now as you read this. And just as what Willis Harmon called "raging tides of chaotic change" seem unbearable, and savagery seems to be the only answer to survival, along come conversations issuing forth from voices that have a clearing and healing effect on the world. Light dawns and major shifts occur in the way life is experienced.

I am speaking not only of the prophets, of Buddha, of Jesus, of Mohammed, of the Founding Fathers of this nation, but also of countless lesser known scientist-philosophers, all speaking and urging Humanity toward a world of brotherhood and Light. From such as these, from committees of correspondence, from chat rooms on the internet, from the work of creative artists, musicians, actors, and writers, breakthroughs are occurring. And in all of the action sanity is breaking out.

It is important to honor the order of things. From light to language to action to form to stasis, to "death" and back to light. And on the frontier where the light is ever present and the darkness appears so formidable, the breakthroughs continue. On the frontier where the light becomes language and language enters time and becomes conversation, the result is what I said, transformation and the possibility of a civilization becoming.

The Day the Lying Stopped

You would think that there would have been a time of great talking, of explanations of how it once was necessary to lie and to defend ourselves and to look good.

But no, the lying just stopped. All the explanations in the world would not have changed one iota the lies themselves or actuality itself spinning out through time, scattered and tangled in what we called past. It was as though there were some profound intervention at work and there was only now and forever to be alive in—and time became a limiting thing. Time became boxes containing shards of actuality, shards of facsimiles swept up into the boxes with no order to them.

From the day when the lying stopped it was acceptable to be silent when we encountered one another. Or, we tended to speak softly, sharing the small wonders that did indeed explode into the moment, into the moment, into the moment.

How had we managed to remain in contact at all during the long eras of the lie? It was as though we each lived in separate rooms of time with adjoining walls composed of approximations of how it was. These constructs formed walls covered with two-sided images, more or less the same, yet self-serving, just as agreements and treaties used to be.

The rule in those days was this: in order to share adjoining walls, two or more had to each alter that which was actually so. This alteration resulted in a facsimile which we adjusted into a more or less common yet self-serving wall. We related to one another then in a kind of tenuous tacit conspiracy, separated from actual contact with one another in the semblances of time called past, present and future, each resulting from the other. All that we perceived and communicated about would then be altered to maintain a semblance of adjoining walls. We soon learned that this process of alteration had to be rigidly maintained, for that which was not altered could not be added to the wall. That which was not altered spun

The Day the Lying Stopped

away into the actual past, leaving open space and light and the possibility of contact, real contact in the light—now and now and now.

Now and again there would be individuals who refused to alter what was so according to the rules, and walls would come down. When this took place, others, a few or great crowds, would gather and, wall-less, the chaos of love and laughter ensued. As at Golgotha and Tiananmen, The Authority did away with them, of course.

Then one day the altering process ceased to be important. It began in several geographical areas at more or less the same time. Not all of the earliest wall droppers, as we now call them, have been interviewed, but a common denominator is that two or more with adjoining walls spontaneously stopped altering and of course their walls began to peel away and whisk out into space. These two or more found themselves wall-less and connected in a kind of lighted dance, at once alone and yet connected in the Light which shone on them and from them. It was as though each had declared, "I am the light. I am what is so. What I say is what is so and we two or more can co-create the world in and from the light of us."

Once the process began it accelerated and spread until now there are only isolated places where the walls still stand, all but overwhelmed, abandoned one by wall-less one, and crumbling in the increasing light.

Attack

Attack—verbal, physical, national as in war, silent as in covert hostility—all are products of profound inner conviction that there is danger out there and one's survival is at stake. The source of such conviction is fear and guilt.

In our crazy world the answer to attack is defense. The best defense is an effective attack, preferably preemptive, i.e., attack first. Of course the thing to do is be prepared for attack always. This is done by practicing what-if, mentally going over what you'll say and do when "they" say and do this or that. As a result there are inner war games, personal war games, family, group and national war games. Thus we live out our crazy lives.

What if? What if we were to perceive that an attack is an appeal for help? What if we were to acknowledge that the essence of help is love—the acceptance of another just the way the other is?

What if we were to perceive that fear and guilt, which are the motivators of attack, are always in the past? What if we knew and could demonstrate that the past has to be constantly reconstructed in present time in order to persist as a factor in our inner and outer lives?

What would happen to our relationships if we took the following stand:

From this moment forward I will be constantly alert to my thoughts of guilt/fear and attack. As these erupt (and they will), I will assign them to the past, wherever—and if—they belong. (Sometimes we are carrying the guilt and fear of other people as though it were our own—for example, being guilty about the slave trade or dropping the atom bomb.) About my own real past I will say, "That was then; this is now." About the past of other people I will also say, "That was then; this is now," thus letting the events go from present time, where they do not really exist.

This act of letting go of events, errors, injustices, wrongs, rights, victories and defeats, casting them off from the present and relegating them to the past where they belong, is what forgiveness is.

Being over-mindful of past successes may well be the source of the pride which goeth before a fall. What if every thought of guilt/fear/attack were converted immediately to forgiveness by my choice? And what if I chose to open to each new endeavor unrestricted by patterns of past success? And what if you chose that, too. And you? And you?

Where would the motive to attack come from if we were clear of the images which we re-create from the past? The City of Sarajevo in the former Yugoslavia became a place where the many Balkan ethnic groups managed very well to live and work together. The winter Olympic games held there in 1984 showed the world a model of ethnic harmony. Since then, haunted by the specters of past atrocities, much of Yugoslavia is now in ruins, and ethnic hatred is rampant, fanned deliberately by gangs of ultra-nationalists. For a few brief years in Sarajevo the past was left in the past and people prospered, ate together, danced and enjoyed their common humanity. Now, enthralled by the horrors of a brutal past, many wonderful people are being kept apart by armed men from other countries lest they slaughter one another, driven again by guilt and fear of attack. They don't know that by directing their attention on the past, they are recreating it in their present lives.

Individually, we humans can redirect our attention from the past to now. From now, we can create what we will. Groups can and have done so in the past. May the truth of that dawn soon among the beautiful people of the Balkans, of the Middle East, of all of the geographical entities whose people are still in the thrall of attack/defend/retaliate.

The Enemy Game

I postulate that enemies do not actually exist. They never have existed. They never will exist. I propose that the idea of enemy is the ultimate craziness.

What say? What about the man down the road who shot your dog? And what about you, you say? What about your ex-wife who ran off with the truck driver and then sued you for divorce on the grounds of desertion and made it stick—and took the house, the car and the kids? What about lawyers and judges, all of them, you say?

Who? Oh! What about Hitler? What about criminals? What about Arabs, Nazis, Communists, Republicans, Jews, Democrats, KKKs, Liberals and Socialists? Okay! What I hear you say is that there are enemies; everybody has enemies. You say I have to believe in enemies or I'm the one who is crazy. Okay. I hear you. Everyone you know or have ever heard of, has enemies. Therefore, there are enemies.

I ask you to consider this. I propose that the reality of enemies, while rampant and endemic among us humans, is an agreement among us; it is a constructed idea. It has to be constantly energized and re-energized and bought and sold among us. I propose we have created an enemy game, and have gotten so involved in it we have forgotten we invented it.

Stop! Wait! Hear me out. You don't have to believe me! And I absolutely refuse to be your enemy; you will have to create me so. Please, just consider this. You don't have to buy it. Okay? Okay.

Where are you now? I mean right now? Look around you.
Where is the man who shot your dog?
Where are you now?
Is the man who shot your dog here with you? Where is he?
Where are you now? Look around you.

Here you are, in your own place and space. And here I am, too. And remember, I have refused to be the enemy. Wouldn't it be crazy to see the man down

The Enemy Game

the road who shot your dog, right here now, as though he were here with us? Wouldn't it be crazy to bring him and an event which happened years ago into our space right now? Is he really here because you see him on your enemy screen in your mind's eye? Well, I propose that re-energizing that man and that event from the past is a crazy thing to do. No, I didn't say you are crazy, because I know that you are not. I say you have projected an enemy into your living space, that's all. The man and the event are not actually here. You with your own creative power have created him and placed him here.

Is he real? No, of course not! Are the feelings you have when you "see" him here, real? Well, they are the feelings you have toward an enemy, toward one who has done wrong, in your eyes. They are as real as he is, here and right now.

Let's turn on the television. Ah! the news. There on the screen is Saddam Hussein, the late tyrant of Iraq. Now there is an enemy. He is real, right?

Okay. Turn off the TV. Where is the enemy? Ah—you "see" him still, you say. Where? Is he here with you right now? Where is the man down the road who at one time shot your dog? Oh then, where is Saddam? I hear you say they are both here. Where? I don't see them. I see you, my friend! I see that you are experiencing the presence of enemies right now. But only you and I are here, and we are friends. We are brothers. I postulate and energize the fact that right now, here, there are no enemies. They do not exist in this right-now time and place. They never really can nor will exist right now. And not ever, unless we postulate and energize them—unless we recreate them.

What did you say? Oh. You do see that enemies aren't really here right now. But you insist that enemies do exist someplace out there. You say there are people out there keeping people hostage. Yes, there was the Holocaust. Yes, some people of every ethnic and "religious" persuasion are plotting murder and terrorizing fellow humans whom their leaders designate as belonging to an axis of evil or the Great Satan. And some Arabs are blowing up Israelis and Israelis are daily killing Palestinians. You might say, to paraphrase the song, that "Everybody hates somebody sometime."

Wait a minute—wait a minute! I thought we turned off the TV. Are all these things happening here? No, of course it is not happening right here. But it is happening, you say. You "see" it, don't you, even though "it"—these ideas and images—are not really here. And you, right now, feel anger and sympathy and feel urged and obligated to take sides and pick and choose enemies and allies out of all this. Don't you?

Okay. You have this marvelous creative power to energize and bring into your right now place of being, images of wars, rumors of wars, enemies, "sides" of conflicts with which you identify. You have the power to bring the Holocaust, the Apocalypse and the whole of the biblical Revelations here into this room. You can feel tormented, threatened, afraid, hateful—real feelings which you can really feel right now. Such power you have! And you can transmit those images across space. You can broadcast those images and their feelings to all who will share them—and they are legion!

I ask you to notice, friend: I have come to visit you, to share friendship, to extend light to light with you, my brother. I come to share what is real with you. I do not choose to project enemies and add my energy to conflicts and thus experience hate and fear with you. All of that is not real; you are projecting it here. It isn't actually here.

I am actually here. And you are actually here, my brother.

For an experiment please shut down your projector. You can start it up again when you will. But just now only, shut it down.

Ah! How quiet it is. Thank you. Yes, the sun is nice, filtering through the trees and into the room. The sounds of birds, of breathing, of laughter somewhere close—harmony. Everything is lighted, in and out. Thank you, light.

What if we extended this Light—sent it out like smiles go out, to all individuals, wherever one is quiet, wherever one has shut the projector down, and (why not?) to all who have not done so?

I postulate and energize a world in the light. And, right now, only the lighted world is real, as it has always been and always will be.

A Giant's Strength

"O, it is excellent to have a giant's strength, but it is tyrannous to use it like a giant." Shakespeare's words so often have contemporary meaning even hundreds of years after they were written.

It seems to me that we who have the good fortune to live in America have an opportunity to cause a major transformation in the way we humans go about survival in this world. If we step back and look out to include our lovely little planet and humanity at large we see that we have gotten ourselves stuck in patterns of consciousness based upon the conviction that it is legitimate and necessary to use our creative power as force in order to have our way with, and to dominate, fellow human beings whom we judge to be evil, errant, even less than human.

The Old Testament presented to humanity the proposition that what we put forth comes back to us equal in force and opposite in direction. This was often stated as "an eye for an eye and a tooth for a tooth, a hand for a hand and a foot for a foot." If you put out my eye, I will put put out yours. These words and many like them have been taken as instructions from on High, making it legitimate for sibling, clan, ethnic, religious and national rivalries to be carried on into future generations. And yet, if this advice is considered to be valid, it is demonstrated to be a fallacy in every direction we look, including the wisdom passed to us in the Sermon on the Mount and other enlightened teachings. I prefer to hear this not as advice on what to do when facing an adversary, but what not to do, lest conflict go on forever.

Of course we had to stop Hitler, but it is well to recognize that his power came from old-way mass consciousness. Not only in Germany, Japan, the Axis powers was brute force considered legitimate. We all, Axis and Allies alike, participated in a belief system which justified mass destruction and the slaying of civilian populations. At the end of World War II the mesmerized people of the Axis were defeated in classical old-way style, by old-way mesmerized Allies.

Then something amazing—transformative—occurred. The victorious Allies (USSR excepted), rather than impose crushing reparations on the Axis nations, chose not to. Instead, Germany, Italy and Japan were allowed to arise up from the rubble to rebuild the ruined infrastructures and subsequently to prosper and to flourish.

This brought about a long period of world prosperity. For the first time in history, responsibility, not spoils, went to the victor. It must be noted that this prosperity did not, and has not, benefitted the millions of humanity who barely managed to subsist in Africa, Asia, the Middle East and the Americas.

The old ways still dominate how we fellow humans use our creative power to serve personal, corporate, and national interests. Our leaders snarl and threaten to punish their leaders and those who follow those leaders. There are now literally millions of our fellow human beings who want to live better lives, who instead must dodge and duck and scramble for bare survival while the thunderbolts of brute power crush homes and cities to rubble. Eyes and teeth trade back and forth in a ghoulish exchange called collateral damage. Who, at this late date, really believes these are effective means of eradicating evil, or even putting it off for a generation or so?

My purpose here is to suggest that there must be a better way for us humans to operate in this world. I propose that there is an entire array of better ways.

I have no doubt that there are many individuals throughout the world who have grown past the chip-on-the-shoulder, line-in-the-sand consciousness which motivates most violent actions. They are no longer addicted to violence as a means of settling disputes. Nor would they favor mass destruction as a means of keeping the peace. All over this planet they are saying to one another, "There must be a better way." This is not spoken of much in the news, but individuals are saying it in letters to friends, and on the internet. More and more books are being published that open minds and hearts to our human possibilities. The word "transformation" shows up wherever those possibilities are considered rather than the normal "ain't it awful" chatter that dominates our "news." Oprah speaks of the possibility of this nearly every day, to tens of millions of people world wide. Spontaneous gatherings of people in their homes and meeting halls are being called together by such organizations as Humanity's Team, where they gather to study and give expression to the urge to become all that it means to be human. Or, as stated by Humanity's Team, to re-create anew the grandest version of the greatest vision ever held about who we are as Human Being. For sure, it is blowing in the wind.

A Giant's Strength

If ever there were a time when it becomes possible to transform the way we go about making life work on this planet, we are in that time. It seems that the flow of history and the means of communication and the planet-wide presence among us of a significant number of thoughtful, altruistic world citizens—scientists, artists, spiritually in-tune men and women and especially young people—have combined to make it possible to put down the old ways and create the new. No longer would we be marching under the old battle flags. Instead we would dance under banners such as harmony, cooperation, sharing and reverence for life.

Key Values To Transform Our Political Conversation in the World
A Statement on Who We Are

We are human beings. We are composite creatures. Each of us is that which is "I," individual and autonomous and yet connected and related in spirit as sibling beings. We have always been so. At our very core we operate out of time, as in now; as in eternity. When we operate in the physical universe, in time, we do so via the bodies of the species Homo sapiens. Most of us also operate our bodies as though the body-with-a-name is really all that we are. While we are persuaded of this we come from a little "i," an ego, an entity which is utterly convinced it is alone and separated and in danger from "all those others." Thus we live out our lives involved in an ongoing "enemy game," forming alliances, creating power structures and misusing our creative power as force against one another. The result of this limited view of who we are comprises the tragic components of the history of the human race.

The questions of who we are and how we came to be have been argued and killed over for millennia. We propose that it is good to hold this question open and to use disciplined quiet moments each day to explore, personally, who we are and to do so in the spirit of "there is always more, and our possibilities border on magnificence." It is not our right to impose beliefs on others which our own self discovery has brought us to see as our "only way." Who we are is answered in the process of self discovery. At last it will be seen that there is no "only way." Ours is just another way. Nor is there a right way and a wrong way, for that is established by whether or not the way works for you, your family, your group, your nation and all of mankind. If your way also works in relation to the environment of vegetable life and animal life and the universes of matter, energy, space and time, why then, go for it and offer to share it. But do not impose it on others nor seek to make them wrong for walking on another path. Again, ours is not the only way ours is but another way. Let workability in the living of life be the standard of comparison.

Individual Autonomy:
The Focal Point of Our Power

We propose that the ages-long patterns of dominance/submission are replaceable in the context of a culture based on free will and the freedom of the individual to follow his or her bliss.

We humans have a history of misuse of our creative power as force and believe that force is justifiable if used for right causes. This belief in all its forms, from blaming and guilt-making to terrorism and war, is a major barrier to the experience of our innate individual autonomy and freedom to be.

We therefore declare our autonomy as individuals and thus must grant that autonomy to all others. In so doing we find it necessary to eliminate from our conversation language which would exclude and prejudge and incite the use of force against any group, race, gender, class, religious belief or other social division. Our conversation will therefore turn toward the unlimited possibilities that we are as human beings. In our conversation we will lay down the habit of creating enemies and making people wrong, and evolve toward making the world work in service to all of us. As individuals we are creative and powerful and each one of us yearns to use that creativity and power for the benefit of self and family and group and nation and all of mankind. Any endeavor or service on which we align ourselves attracts the creative and powerful participation of others, for it is true that two or more gathered generate energies greater than the sum of the energies of the individuals involved.

Any endeavor or service on which individuals align attracts the creative and powerful participation of others, for it is true that two or more gathered generate energies greater than the sum of the energies of the individuals involved. When an idea or intention takes root in one, and is agreed to by one other, a dynamic synergy then attracts others. It is said of such a process, "There is no force as powerful as an idea whose time has come." This process, allowed to accelerate, can become the engine for changes such as the movements for independence by the American colonies and the people of India under the guidance of Mohandas Gandhi, and the Civil Rights movement in America. The power generated by such movements comes from the alignment of individual intention, writ large by the fact that every individual is endowed by the Creator with creativity and power and autonomy.

Environmental Stewardship

We acknowledge and accept that this planet is a self-perpetuating commonwealth from which can be derived, through our conscious and caring stewardship, all that is needed to provide food, clothing and shelter for our Homo sapiens creatures. We human beings are stewards of this outflowing of supply and we are free to work in harmony with the laws of motion by which that outflowing continues. Stewardship implies the conscious willing co-operation of free individual human beings aligned toward optimum use of the environment. Private ownership can be and often is an exercise of stewardship. When that ownership expands and consolidates into monopoly, cartel and state collective, stewardship, which is based on individual autonomy, is subverted.

We are human beings and we share a small but well-provisioned planet from which we derive an ample sustenance and have done so for millennia. From time to time earthquakes and weather patterns have brought about imbalances so that the overall abundance of the Earth is not experienced by all the creature bodies on it. It is a paradox that just when we have achieved the ability to quickly bring to balance such natural imbalances, we have managed to come up with ways to artificially generate imbalances which are every bit as devastating as earthquakes and volcanoes, if slower and not so dramatic. These artificial imbalances are depressions, recessions and inflations. They are also wars over land and ideologies and they all manifest in the use of our creative power as force against our fellow human beings. These imbalances result from a deep conviction held by nearly all of us that, actually, the supply of life support on this planet is not sufficient, that there is not enough for all. Those who are presently the have-nots are utterly convinced that the haves are at fault for not sharing their over-abundance. The haves, also sure that there isn't enough, feel obliged to grasp their wealth and power more closely to them. For survival, of course—for their families, for their class, for their nation and the practices and ways of being that make up, for them, "our way of life."

We declare that it is a false notion that there is not enough on this planet to go around. Natural scarcities brought about by natural disasters can be brought to balance quickly and efficiently. Only little "i," family, national and arbitrary economic barriers, (all ego Homo sapiens considerations) prevent this. It is pointless to seek out who is to blame for these barriers because all that need be done is for each of us, one by one, to change our minds about the specter of perpetual scarcity.

We declare that there is no scarcity. Creative, responsible use of the resources of the planet is possible. That is a global fact. It requires only acknowledgement and the creative action that would flow therefrom.

Global Responsibility

Our responsibility is world wide because our human being is world wide. Every individual autonomous being is responsible for the condition of this world and the people in this world. No one is exempt from that. There is no "them" to blame for those conditions which render our lives less than they could be. What we see and experience is an outworking of our aggregate conversation in the world. Because this is so, it is not appropriate that any of us march forth as liberators of others. To do so requires that we are convinced and would convince others that they are not free. Instead we call for and align our creative power with all those everywhere who come from the knowledge of their own freedom. There is a profound difference between the actions of liberators and the actions of those who acknowledge their freedom and the innate freedom of all human beings. We say, "Beware the liberators for they must first convince you that you are not responsible and are thus victims and must be liberated."

We are responsible. Our world is shaped by our conversation in it. We are not victims and all human beings are free.

Human Rights

A profound statement is made in the Declaration of Independence of the United States of America: "We hold these truths to be self evident, that all men are created equal, that all men are endowed by the Creator with certain inalienable rights; these rights are life, liberty and the pursuit of happiness." Somehow these rights have been added to, and what were acknowledged as endowments of the Creator now include entitlements which are in fact individual and aggregate responsibilities of all human beings.

Each one of us has been created as an individual free spirit. We live and have the right to declare what our happiness is and to go for it. Each of us is responsible for how we go about achieving our happiness. We are responsible for the quality of how we live our lives. The quality of our lives is what we choose to make of life. The quality of our lives is not a matter of rights. It is a reflection of where and how we direct our powerful attention. As human beings we have been endowed with the power of creative attention. We are endowed with the ability to align our attention with others. Such alignment results in an exponential increase of our power to create the quality of life of those so aligned, and to a degree, even of those non-aligned by choice or fear or ignorance or simply because they have chosen other values. We are endowed with certain powers. All that we experience for good or ill is a direct product of how we use these powers.

We hear politicians say that every human being is entitled to whatever quality and quantity of health care, nutrition, shelter, economic security, relevant education, meaningful and rewarding work, full reproductive rights, child care and a safe and healthy environment are deemed by him to be desirable. Politicians may get our votes for saying such things, but both the promiser and the voter are confusing entitlements with responsibilities.

We say that every human being has been created with the power to create for himself, with his family, with his community and with and for all of mankind whatever quality and quantity of health care, nutrition, shelter, economic security, relevant education, meaningful and rewarding work, full reproductive rights, child care and a safe and healthy environment, are deemed by them to be desirable. These are not entitlements to be expected to come to us from sources outside ourselves and independent of our contribution. They are ours for the creating in alignment with others who freely choose to align.

Toward a Creative Politics

Politics, as we ego/Homo sapiens practice it, is essentially a continuation of war by other means. Our political conversation is adversarial in the extreme. The fact that governments manage to operate at all, given the continuous barrages of attack/defend by which they carry on, attests to the strength and steadiness of a handful of individuals who manage to rise above the clamor and cause to be done what has to be done. This near miracle of small centers of sanity amid the turbulence also shows up in families, corporations, church congregations, neighborhood taverns, coffee klatches, PTAs—wherever two or more gather. We declare that the fractious, blaming and defensive way of being in politics is not only wasteful and dangerous to the survival of the planet, it simply is not necessary.

Key Values To Transform Our Political Conversation in the World

We declare that, as it is with all else in this bountiful universe, there is, for the creating, a very nearly infinite array of better ways.

There are certain realities that it would be wise to acknowledge. When any one of us is fearful and frozen in the run/attack mode, we are incapable of seeing anything but danger and enemy. Further, when we are fearful, angry, covert, apathetic, resigned, bored, antagonistic and judgmental we are incapable of being creative, friendly or aware of other possibilities. Bluntly, when we operate in the modes and conversations coming forth from such emotional miasmas we are not sane and we are dangerous to ourselves and to each other. In fact, war, racial and ethnic genocide, secret governments, and racism are the continuation of politics arising from such means.

Our human political history attests to the verity of the above. And there have been times and there have been gatherings of remarkable men and women who have operated from sanity, from dignity, from respect for others and from creativity, and who have generated means for the evolution of governments and civilizations which made sanity and the human possibility become manifest on our small planet, if only for a time.

We declare that sanity is always a possible choice to be made. We call upon those who are willing to forgo the habit of the enemy game and commit themselves to create a new Human alignment which transcends the turmoil of politics and is based upon the magnificent possibilities of being human beings alive and conscious here on this planet at this time. Such a call has been made by an organization with which this writer has aligned: Humanitiy's Team.

Sanity is a Matter of Choice

Realities and world views which are fear based are not sane. Any reality in which is postulated the constant existence of enemies is not sane. Listen to the conversations going on around us. Listen to our own conversations, our contributions to the apparent presence of fear and want and enemy. Know that, with rare moments of exception, our conversation in the world is not sane.

We propose that each of us take note of those moments when we are not participating in insane conversation. What is it that we are doing with our attention when not so involved? Are we attending to a beautiful sunset? A baby's smile? A kitten being a kitten? Attending to one that we love? Being grateful and appreciative of the moment being experienced? The warmth of the sun; the pleasure of a warm shower or a relaxing bath? The pleasure of movement of the body in dance or accomplishment of art or work or game, or making love with one that we love? Being in the presence of great works of art: music, drama, paintings, sculptures, poems? These are moments of sanity. These are moments when the apparency of fear and need and enemy does not exist. We take note of that. We acknowledge that. These are moments seemingly out of time. They often come as a surprise, and they last until we again attend to the conversations of fear, need and enemy.

We declare that the essential act that transforms our political conversation from the adversarial habit that is now extant in the world to a conversation of sanity and even joy is a simple matter of choice. The choice is for sanity which is experienced as creative power, as expansiveness, as altruism—just that simple choice for. Or, as Shakespeare's Hamlet posed it, "To be, or not to be, that is the question."

This choice and the declaration of this choice creates an opening for all the possibilities there are in being human. The simple act of alignment which such a declaration evokes, brings about an exponential empowerment of those so aligned. When two or more are so gathered, empowered transformation occurs. In the context of such a transformation, the specters of fear, need and enemy disappear from the conversation, and the politics of possibility take form.

We say that this does not have to be believed to be experienced. Yet it does have to be chosen and declared. The power of such a choice and declaration is such that the experience of transformation must follow.

"We"......The above declaration was written in 1988. At that time there was no group in mind when I used the word "we." I did yearn for an alignment of others in sync with these values. That was then. Now, fifteen years later, a huge change has taken place and what was only yearning is now showing up world wide among many organizations that have come into being since this was written.

Ego and I

Whatever is of the ego is reactive, combative, limiting and contracting, as in "gimme-gimme-gimme," as in "I'll take mine before it's all gone." To the ego, it is a certainty that there is not enough supply to go around, and that all others are the enemy or the necessary allies against the enemy. Whatever is of the ego converts value into detriment, altruism into sympathy, smiles of sharing, of enjoyment, into grins of derision.

Whatever is of expanding consciousness is of that which is I, human being, child of the Creator. Whatever is of expanding consciousness is inclusive, unlimited, alive with possibilities, alive with goodwill toward our sibling children of God. Human being seeks to add who he is to the action, to make things work better, to enhance, to bring forth what is missing and render it beautiful.

I make these statements as declarations. I do not offer proof because I have no proof that can be consistently replicated in the perception of another, or of my perception, for that matter. There are moments of my life in which I am inclusive, unlimited, alive with possibilities, alive with goodwill toward my sibling children of the Creator. At such moments I am alive as in no other time. And somehow those moments have permanence, as though they are out of time. Like now. Like forever.

There have been days and decades in my life over which ego has had apparent control. Such days can be days of scarcity or affluence, but they are always days of hunger for recognition and control and power over others, for ego ever desires to be king. There have been days of rebellion, of "down with the king," for the ego also ever desires to overthrow those who are envied, the fat cats, the centers of apparent power, which continually wax and wane in their potency as projected in the perceptions of egos. As ego I know I am alone and defenseless, surrounded by enemies and therefore must unite with other egos (as much as I distrust them) to construct fortresses of power and tools for the destruction of those enemies.

There are days and decades of egodom in contrast to only moments of expanding consciousness, of human being. One thing I can say with certainty is that there is a difference and I know the difference when the experience is upon me. I also know that it is most desirable to change that ratio of decades of egodom and only moments of human being to at least days and hours of human being and only moments of egodom—to move from the loneliness of ego to individual autonomy and thus willingness for cooperation in the world of human being.

I am also increasingly certain that such a transformation can be chosen, and that the opportunities, examples and coaches are in place and available to each of us. I say coaches, rather than teachers, for it becomes ever more clear that this transformation is a matter of practice, which can be affected by coaching.

Information, which has been poured forth for centuries from pulpits and academic podia and books and now by all our present day marvelous media, seems not to have been readily converted to practice and thus become knowledge. Instead it has more often been ego-converted to superstition and to provide rationales for combat, tyrannical power games and games of rebellion. I think we can say with some certainty that information becomes knowledge only in practice, in living life itself.

Also, I think that this is a time of transformation, and the opportunity for conscious practice is there for each of us. Probably the opportunity has always been there. Certainly the quest has always been there but I think that now more individuals are open to it. It is as though a significant minority of human being has come awake, is looking about to find that there are others, in an exponentially increasing number, the very light of whom is generating further awakening.

Coaches, mentors, trainers and tutors operate one-on-one with individual attention given to the practice, to the actual results. Their work is most often done in relation to individuals who have requested their services. Such individuals have found themselves suddenly awake and on a quest and willing to accept guidance. Such willingness, if acknowledged, never goes unfulfilled. It is important to realize that these coaches, these providers of light, can come in many guises. It is also well to understand that they are strongly disinclined to operate where they have not been invited. To interfere is, to them, to do disrespect to the free will of human being. The old saying is, "When the pupil is ready, the teacher is waiting." I would rather say that when a person is in motion on the frontier, and face to face with that which he knows not and desires to know, the possibilities and opportunities are there and the desire is as a magnet actively evoking what is appropriate for moving on. And what activates that magnet is but the desire acknowledged and just a little silence, a stillness, a listening—in a word, humility.

That we are all on our frontiers, that we are all on a quest, that we are truly awake and alert to know much that we don't even know that we don't know—these realities are good to acknowledge. That of us which is ego may well be resistive to transformation. But oh! what opportunities there are now for human being! The possibilities! And to think that our coaches are in place, just a Silence away!

Openness

There are mind changes and belief changes now occurring which impact the world conversation toward survival. In the rush of oncoming events it has become apparent that the old dichotomies of belief which now fuel our conflicts, personal, familial, group, national and international, have no use value as a means for causing sustainable survival for any but a privileged few on this lovely small planet.

In this dawning awareness a new polarity of consciousness is emerging. This polarity concerns openness, transparency, integrity, altruism; these, as other than the adversarial polarities to which we have been addicted. This dawning consciousness is characterized by openness and inclusion—as other than (not opposed to) closed awareness and exclusion. We see organizations, societies and nations opening their records, revealing their secrets and, under umbrellas of amnesty and forgiveness, engaging in all manner of cleansings and clearings of murky specters from the adversarial past. Families too are clearing closets of useless skeletons and skewed stories of events long past. Yes, we continue to see attempts here and there to shut down or maintain closed associations and systems and nations.

We are in a period where it is possible to choose individually and as Humanity between closing down our ways of being, or opening to the enormous array of possibilities spread out before us by the individuals who have done the good work in times before. It is showing up in a soil prepared for it by people all over the world who have come to a consciousness wherein anything less than openness is no longer acceptable.

Who are these people who have prepared this soil? They are men and women, parents, grandparents, aunts, uncles, children and friends of the children of our time. These people have common qualities which distinguish them; quiet qualities, discrete, one by one and yet binding them without noise, badges or uniforms. It is as though they are connected across and despite all the old boundaries of nation, race, language, culture and belief structure. This growing population has evolved seemingly spontaneously into networks of leavening centers amidst the cacophony and turmoil of the marketplaces and the battlefields which both attract us and separate us.

These men and women have characteristics which can usually be discerned among them. These are really individual characteristics; their commonality does not manifest uniformly like troops on maneuvers or protesters with their signs. Rather these characteristics manifest uniquely, like works of art; the world somehow richer for them whether or not perceived by the world. Consider these characteristics as some among many.

Beliefs and other forms of popular consensus have been examined and reevaluated by each individual—the false and the useless being discarded, and the useful being personally reformulated and expandable. Always expandable. From such a ground of being one finds scientists who can allow for a Creator and deeply spiritual people who can allow for the expanding horizons of science.

There is an awareness of their own naive antagonism to the new and the alien. And being thus aware they are disinclined to participate in the automaticity of prejudice. They are likewise disinclined to justify the use of their creative power as force to control their fellows. They evolve, instead, a tolerance of and sometimes an appreciation of alien differences. They have a tendency to enfold and allow in rather than insulate and exclude.

Some are formally well-educated and all are self-educated, engaged in an ongoing examination of whatever shows up in their lives, that they realize to the fullest the possibilities of being a human being. They choose to have children or they choose not to have children; choice being the common denominator. Most choose to beget and rear children or to serve that process as nurturer and teacher. All are acutely aware of the necessity of a secure and caring community to provide both opportunity and parameters for the growth of children. They regard children as sentient beings, not toys or pets. At the same time they recognize that the animal Homo sapiens is there to be trained to the point where the human being has a refined tool to work with—child and adult human beings collaborating on this.

Choice is seen by them to be the motivator of what occurs in their lives. You do not hear from one of these that "the universe did it to me." There is a growing appreciation of the creative power of language to bring what is being spoken into living experience. Conversation then is appreciated as the creative exercise it is.

There often is an almost welcoming acceptance of Eros in life—that wild wind in which chaos and cosmos dance among us humans calling us forth to our personal frontiers.

They are in motion, not fixed. They have come to see the limitations of ideology. They are willing therefore to step forth from their belief boxes to examine what is there now, and now. They thus become aware of the magnificent and unfathomable order which actually exists, and align with that.

Almost universally these people have moved off the liberal/conservative (or whatever form this takes in other countries) dichotomy in which one is one and the other be damned—to instead identify with the core reality of their relatedness as human beings. They become the conservators and nurturers, savoring thus the wealth of this small planet and making things work, so that it continues to give forth as it was intended to the generations to come, with no one left out.

These are the people all over this planet who have created and called forth in the living of their lives the nation without boundaries or barriers in which openness lives.

Addiction to Violence

It hit me hard. After decades of thinking I had resolved my anger and tendency to violent behavior, here it came again. It was only a few years ago. Saddam Hussein initiated an invasion of Kuwait. George Bush declared there to be a line in the sand. My first reactions to both of these insanities was cold anger. "Damn!! Saddam Hussein shouldn't get away with this!" Then, "Damn it! George Bush and the military are drumming up a slaughter." Only a day or so after those reactive outrages did I realize that I was a participant—that I, too, was projecting images of violence and punishment, first to the Iraqis and then to what to me was the saber rattling of too many of our leaders. I had not yet confronted that there was a generic warrior in myself. For a brief time there I remembered the Alamo, the Maine, Pearl Harbor. I replayed in some secret viewing room of mind or soul news posters depicting Germans in spiked hats bayoneting Belgian babies, and other ghastly atrocities, bodies piled on bodies like so much offal, images of which and worse may well be carried in our genes. Certainly they are carried on the evening news and certainly they take living form in that worldwide "inner" conversation we share with all others on the planet.

As I became reluctantly aware that the warrior reactions were mine as well as Saddam Hussein's and George Bush's, I began to be ashamed that here in the smoke and flame of arcade-like slaughter, I shared the desire to see harm done to others. It was then that I realized, Pogo-like, that the enemy is as a mole lurking in our secret spaces and the mole is an extension of ourselves. All right, damn it! The mole is an extension of myself. As I said, this realization hit me hard. Condemn George Bush for pompous warmongering? There, I saw myself. React to the cruel and ancient tribal dominance of others by Saddam Hussein? What else is new? I felt that way too! I felt cruel desire to harm the Iraqi gang of Hussein. Then it became clear to me. There is no end to this monstrous cruelty let loose in this world unless and until I find its roots in myself. When I speak of violence here I speak of verbal and emotional violence as well as physical violence. I speak of sarcasm and snide put-downs and racist snarls and other such assault weaponry of the mind. I call attention to this ugly subject because I believe that there is a way out.

I propose that there is a "place" within the consciousness of each of us that functions as the launching pad for our violent behavior as individuals and as nations. This "place" is an internal screening studio where it is possible to review and re-experience whatever joys, sorrows, betrayals, defeats and victories have accrued in our lives. Here also we can project composite experience culled from our reading, from misunderstood stories heard in our childhood, from movies and from the incessant gossip and chatter of coffee klatches and evening news. Here, too, we carry on our silent conversations in the world, conversations rife with political, racial and religious judgments, condemnations that "they're all alike," "you can smell the garlic" and "they breed like flies"; terms like "jack-booted government agents," "skinheads," "militiamen," "tax-and-spend liberals" and "mean-spirited conservatives."

It is also true that the screening room is available to uplift and enlighten those who would use it thus. Paul counseled the Philippians on the desirability to think on (we would now say projections) "whatsoever things are honest....just, whatsoever things are lovely.....of good report...." We, too, can think on these things, but it is my sad observation that the habit is to seek out more "interesting" (read violent or titillating) fare. Given the choice between barbarism and civilization we choose the excitement of the former and I propose that we do so out of ignorance of the beauty and the joy potential of living civilized and creative lives.

Civilization. All through my life I have had the notion that there is a grand human destiny, a purpose that expresses the magnificent creating power that we are as human being. I don't know where that notion comes from. There have been voices that would hand me that notion in an ideological package. Other voices have sought to tell me that such an idea is foolish, naive, idealistic. I have listened to those voices and I often can see and hear the logic and the reasonableness of what they are saying. This, especially after a dose or two of news of Bosnia or Chechnya or the previous night's shootings in our American cities. Yet there are other moments, sublime moments: Bach pouring forth from piano or voice, or one of those moments of reconciliation which have brought such hope to the peacemakers of our world. I am still brought to tears by the memory of Anwar Sadat standing before the Israeli Knesset and speaking—offering actually—the possibility of peace in our time. And Gorbachev's visit to St. Paul and Minneapolis, and Nelson Mandela, and the fall of the wall! And lesser known people of our time who stood and stand still, steady in the light: A cellist who plays daily on the streets of Sarajevo comes to mind. He plays as a reminder that the light remains on despite the barbarians, those forgetful ones booming and blasting at one another in the hills above the crumbling and bleeding city.

Sarajevo, Rwanda, Chechnya, where the ancient hatreds burst forth and consume the living with lava-like persistence. They are there on our collective video screens. By their presence we know that barbarism is possible. And yet, somehow there is still this grand notion of our human destiny which seems forever formed, even tangled with the light, the silence, the center of who I am as human being; who we all are as human being. Always, if there is this light, this silence, this center within me, then I know it there in you and all human kind. I cannot hold such a notion as one alone. That is so. Thus, civilization is possible.

Civilization is something that is formed within me. This form within me is something I yearn for and it is something that I sense is already in place. I cannot tell you where that near certainty comes from. Quite the reverse seems to be so. When one of the explaining voices speaks of the Kingdom of God, I "see" this civilization which has formed in me. I sign on to the Usonian dream of Frank Lloyd Wright, of buildings functional yet growing where they erupted from the designer's joy, scattered like seeds to grow in friendly nestings of citizens. I see homes and gardens open to the seasonal light and reflective of the souls alive within and welcoming those afar who are heading home. On every country pathway and city neighborhood I am aware of cleanliness, carefulness, mindfulness of the commonwealth. I see people, active, open, friendly and trusting. I see there are no locks and no police and no armies. The sense of commonwealth enhances rather than diminishes the true individuality of spirit of each citizen. The glorious idea of being Citizen is vibrant in each one. There are children everywhere. They are alive, alert, active and honored and taught as human being, not as puppies or property.

I say that this vision of a civilization even now in place is there to be energized by anyone who will. It only takes remembering and attending to. For me the remembering is often the result of pausing in the moment of being in the presence of beauty, musical performances, paintings, sculpture, poems, theater productions or some utterly beautiful moment of nature, or that moment of recognition between me and another human being delighting both in what this very moment is so, and the forever connections which continue from such moments. These are civilized moments. They come as a surprise, yet in retrospect it seems that they were always there and one can come to expect them, I believe, by simply being out there, alive in the light. That is what is so for me about civilization. It is something I yearn for and as I have said, it seems even now to exist.

Standing between us and this civilization is our conversations of fear and violence that form and swirl around us like some gaseous fog from the past. We are addicted to deliberately entering our viewing rooms and turning up the violence. To say what is so, we have a nearly infinite range of subjects and moods and motions in which to invest our attention. We have friends and families to love, dances to dance, novels and poems to write and read to one another, and all the musics great and small. That our actual choices often tend toward various forms of the enemy game is, I propose, a major cause of our penchant for violence and the use of force to dominate and control one another. It is as though we are addicted to violence—drawn to it almost helplessly even though it is terribly harmful to ourselves, our families, our fellow human beings and other life forms on this planet. Harmful to the degree that our potential to live civilized lives on our ample little planet seems in real jeopardy. And much of our violence is hidden, even from ourselves. It is potential violence, as nuclear ICBMs are potential, to be fired off by choice, or not, but motivated, always, by "them," over there. Again, in parallel with the patterns associated with addiction, we hide our violence, we deny it and thus it festers and builds up pressure. While it is true that our creative power makes it possible to experience what we put our attention on, it is also true that we continue to experience that which we deny as being our responsibility. Our choice to deny that we participate in violence has the same power and the same results as our choice to fulminate and rage.

It is this covert violence, this private violence, which perpetuates the fear we walk around in; this fear which in turn generates defensiveness and plans for pre-emptive violence. Just listen to the militiamen. Just listen to the world leaders. And it is this inner violence which each of us can unhook from. Unhook from, of course, after we admit that we generate these violent inner conversations, and after we acknowledge that they turn on automatically, seemingly unbidden. Unhook from, that is, after we acknowledge further that we call them up out of our past and can let them recede into the past with only a few seconds of pause needed to let them go. I need to be careful here. I acknowledge that it is very easy to say such things and I claim no authority to do so other than that I have managed, now and again, to do it. It is not yet fail-safe for me but it has been my experience that it is possible and downright relieving to practice this pause before the patterned blast-off occurs. The main barrier to its practice is that it is so simple that anyone can do it. And it is so for me that this addiction and its barbaric results can be dealt with like any of our other addictions about which we have learned so much in recent decades.

Civilization is possible. It simply needs attending to.

An Opinion About Opinions

In a recent conversation with a friend I proposed that much civility could be returned to human discourse if we would get clear in our minds that there is a difference between information and knowledge. I had said that information can become knowledge by actually experiencing what the information presents as a possibility. My friend called me on that proposition and asked me to support my assertion.

Well, for openers: when alert to this difference, one has the opportunity to gain some humility and consequently some peace of mind. In Columbus' time the good people of the Mediterranean regions had a tendency to get excited over the proposition that the Earth was round and not flat as it was previously assumed. It would have been helpful for those Genoese to have been aware that information and opinions are not knowledge. But when Columbus returned after not falling off the edge of the Earth, everybody began the centuries-long process of changing their minds about the shape of our lovely small planet. We have now reached the point where it can be said that nearly half of us now know the reality of the matter. The planet Earth is what it is, a saucer-shaped vessel carried on the backs of four turtles.

The arguments were over opinions. Opinions, after all, are useful in the same way that hypotheses are useful, they open the door of the mind to possibilities. But it is good to know and to acknowledge that one is putting forward opinions and not actualities. And yes, one can operate quite well with information as though it were knowledge, as in following assembly instructions. But consider the importance of one's data base of experience that enables one to do so. (Such is my mechanical data base that I wince at the memory of Christmas eves and my attempts to assemble childrens' play kitchens, etc., following those "easy" instructions.)

My friend went on to say that when our use of language ignores the gradient we can easily escalate controversy, create barriers, muddle our thinking. Our current president skated out onto the thin ice of duality thinking when he declared to the world "If you are not with us, you are against us." He would have us believe that there are only two options when there is an array of options in the considerable gradient space available to our right to choose. And not only to choose what others are offering, but also to create any number of better ways, thus expressing the noble mantle of Citizen.

Then my friend asked me to define wisdom. I risked this definition. If knowledge is information and data that is used to the point that it can be experienced, then wisdom is the balanced, practical and appropriate use of that knowledge for beneficial-to-mankind purposes. My friend said he felt comfortable with that. The conversation then broadened to the question of whether or not two people, such as ourselves, gathered for the purpose of discourse about information, knowledge and wisdom, could possibly have any impact on others.

I said I thought so, yes. I speak not from knowledge here, but just try it on. I see the two of us as individual "lights," if you will. And all of us, humanity, as one Light. As each of us thinks and languages our way along the frontier of mind and consciousness the individual "lights" get brighter. This is my opinion and an analogy. Yet, at this moment, it is almost palpably real to me. It seems to me that the more we, each of us, apply ourselves to clearer perception of what is so, the more we turn up the light for others. This results in an exponential combining of the light. Somehow the words are the bridge, or the light conduit, and yet the light precedes its conduit. So we acknowledge the light and the conduit and plod, or soar on forward. We are told that Bach inscribed the words "To the glory of God" on each piece of music he composed. Talk about light! Talk about conduit!

The World According to An AARP

I admit to being an AARP, but that does not mean that I want to get something for nothing. I do not. And that, for no other reason than I have come to the certainty that it's not possible. Okay? I mean, I think the world works in such a balance and order that whatever is put forth by each and all of us increases the inflow of whatever that is, and then the increased inflow spills over into spaces that can never be left empty. What I am saying is that the universe provides us individually and collectively with whatever it is that we put forth from our very own selves.

I know this isn't very AARP-like of me to say, but "No, fellow AARPs, there are no entitlements." Therefore, Mr./Ms. lawyer/politician, you do not have the power to grant them or take them away. Look. We get what we are entitled to. We get what we put forth into the world according to the law. No, not lawyers' law—nature's law. Like gravity. If you consider the operation of gravity, you have the law of which I speak. Nature's law.

Where was I? Oh, yeah. AARP, the American Association of Retired Persons. A retired person is one who has no weekends off, no vacations, no salary or wages from gainful employment. That would also describe children before the age of five and those citizens capable of working who are unemployed.

AARP! AARP! Sounds like seals barking. Throw them fish and they clap and toot horns and wear funny hats and nominate images of themselves to run for office and glare at the opposition whenever, rarely, it is possible to tell the opposition apart from their very own selves.

We contemporary AARPS were mostly born after the end of World War I. We were taught by our parents and our civics teachers that that war was the war to end all wars, a war to preserve the world for democracy. That sounded pretty good to some of us and we decided to believe that it was so. Most of us now, after numerous additional wars, are downright cynical about such ideas. A few of us though, well, we still think such things are possible. It seems so obvious that what we have to do is get sane enough to notice that what we put our attention on takes form. I mean we create the life that we are experiencing, and therefore what we are experiencing right now is what we have been attending to. I happen to believe that to be so. No, it doesn't work out unless you apply it to each and all of us past and present. Like gravity works for everybody who operates in gravity's paradigm. In the paradigm of cause and effect, by the way we direct our attention, we cause the experience of our life.

Apparently we AARPs as a class of humanity are afraid to die. I say that because we submit to extraordinary and exotic tortures in order to live a few months longer. Me, I don't exactly delight in the idea of dying, especially now when things are going so well for me. But when I think about death, **my** death, well, I am interested. I expect that right at that moment I'll have a lot of questions answered all at once. Like, Is there life after death? Will I see my mother, my grandmother, my dad, my brother, my sister? I wonder. That would be fun.

Many of us AARPs carry heavy, heavy burdens. Grudges and prejudices so sticky and solidified that we have lost all touch with each other, or the blue skies, or the trees, or the moon waxing and waning in a sea of stars, seeing only, now, the bent and gooey images that we project from the very center of our burdens onto the gummy inner vision screen which serves as our reality. Laughter? Some can still laugh a little, but to many, just to laugh at, not with. And forgotten, too often, is our child laughter, delighted, healing, cosmic.

We AARPs are quite convinced that there is a **they** out there and **they** are to blame. Now I am not saying that all AARPs are alike in the assignment of **they** out there. In fact we differ in the **theys** we blame but we are as one in that we all blame **theys** and for some of us the **theys** include each other. Speaking for myself I must say that there are AARPs who consider Social Security and Medicare for themselves as earned and accrued personal assets, whereas for others, they are entitlements which will send the economy to its doom. This is the kind of logic which cheers the death and destruction of other peoples, their soldiers and their cities and then would destroy the world in "defense of our own." Somehow "our own" human beings are better than, senior to, **them** over there. Hey, fellow AARPs, why is it so nearly impossible for us to recognize that some of us are jerks just as some of them are jerks? Or why do we resist acknowledging that, at times, we are all capable of being magnificent and creative, charitable, loving and forgiving human beings, and other times we are as bestial as the worst of us in history? Most of us who went to war against the "dirty yellow peril" were full of hate and the need for revenge, against all of **them**. Actually it was against our projected images of them fueled by the poisons in our own hearts, as U.S. citizens were marched off to internment camps. In response to my testimony that "I went to school with kids of Japanese parents—every one I knew was a good student, a good citizen and a good friend," too often the devastating retort would come, "Oh yeah? Would you want one of them to rape your sister?"

I remember scratching my head at this, thinking, "Gee, no!" It took some time for me to sort it out that I wouldn't want anyone to rape my sister. And it was another decade or so before I found out that such thoughts and alternatives were projections from the memory and desire banks of the speaker. I doubt that even today one could get away with "No I certainly wouldn't want one of them to rape my sister but now I know the thought of doing so is in **your** heart."

Clear in my mind is the day that one of the navy armed guard came aboard after a few hours ashore. He brought with him a human skull ("It's a Jap," he claimed) which he had found on a recent battlefield—Kwajalein, I think it was. He was so pleased. I was so disgusted with him, with all of us, with me. And yes, it was only a skull—the person was gone and I trust not obliged to witness the scene. No doubt today that sailor is a respectable AARP and proud of his participation in the "Good War."

Somehow we AARPS have lived our lives carelessly in our consideration of the right to life, liberty and the pursuit of happiness of some of the others out there. Of course there are AARPs who do care, who would always be about making the world work for everybody. But the wars and the hatreds drown such voices and then we wonder why the desire for Uzis is so rampant among us. For hunting? Sure......

I learned during that war that it is wise to be discerning of those to whom you would confess your unwillingness to demonize those designated as enemy. Yes, and I learned to choose carefully to whom I would speak of the obscenity of racism so rampant on those ships engaged in a struggle to establish the "Four Freedoms" for all. To speak out for a more balanced and tolerant view of enemies and racial minorities could well put you in hot water aboard most ships I sailed on. Perhaps, and worse, you could find yourself swimming in the cold and lonely water in the wake of your ship.

But then, it could be that such an end is better (just look about you) than to find yourself half alive in the world that our careless attention and and careful silence has now begot.

The Importance of Being Presumptuous

I admit to being presumptuous. That is why I get up most every morning and do these mutterings. I presume there is some value to it. There is value to me in the exercise itself. The strings of words sometimes seem to nudge my frontier out just a little farther. I presumptuously assume that as my frontier expands so does the frontier of human being.

Yes, it is presumptuous to tread in the gardens or territory of those who have credentials and can thus be taken seriously. So I propose, then, that these mutterings not be taken seriously. For tread I will and credentialed I am not. Besides, it has been my observation that being very serious does not bring me to my frontier. The frontier stuff is light, airy. There is laughter and playfulness on the frontier. When I choose miracles instead of wallowing in ego seriousness the choice comes with a chuckle. Then there is the matter of joy, which, by the way is the very opposite of matter. (Not that there is anything wrong with matter—other than its tendency to be stolid and solid and just sit there. Matter is, oh, obvious.) Joy, on the other hand, is seldom where you look. It shows up where you are just about to look. Or, like the movement of twigs where a wild creature just was, joy is mostly just missed. Joy is like now—by the time you register it, it is then. Is it too obvious, too presumptuous to say that joy is now and now is joy?

Yes, probably too presumptuous. Not only that, "Joy is now and now is joy" becomes immediately jelled into concept, and say what you will about concepts, for sure they don't sparkle. They don't live. Concepts are like boxes we put life itself in with the idea that someday we may have some use for it. For example: well, here we are on a rainy day. What's to do? Maybe it would be a good time to open a concept and live what's inside. Hmmm, let's see. Ah, here's one. It is labeled "Joy is now and now is joy." Okay, I'll open it. That's funny; there's nothing in the box. Somebody must have used it already. But it was **my** concept. I found it on December 6, 1987, and I saved it for a rainy day.

The Importance of Being Presumptuous

Profound question. (No, not serious. Profound, like the direct clear look of a baby is profound.) How do we live on the frontier of us, alive, now, joyful—and not immediately start boxing it and hoarding it and looking at where it was and no longer is?

I playfully and prayerfully propose that answers to profound questions are only boxes to put life in for a rainy day. Instead, try this. Simply hold open the question itself. Dance along the edge of the frontier in the question. Dance with what shows up. Let it sparkle from your eyes. Don't grab it, don't save it. Above all, don't take it seriously, it's alive!

See you there!

Transition Times

Each human being, child and adult, saint and criminal is, right now, a child of God. We, human being, are sibling children of the Creator. Therefore, as beings, we are all that we can be. This actuality is what I choose to call our spiritual presence. This is who we are.

Those of us who are currently walking about on this planet, visible to one another, are visible via a creature called Homo sapiens. Homo sapiens is an animal which has been evolved and adapted to function as communication devices and perceptors and tools for human being to operate here in the physical universe. Each of us is a composite entity, child of God/spirit/human being/animal Homo sapiens.

We have been operating this way for millennia. For millennia we have, by and large, considered ourselves to be our Homo sapiens creatures rather than the operators of them. Thus we have separated ourselves from who we are in the mistaken consideration that we are only these animal creatures.

We also retained a deep-seated sense that we were more than that animal creature and, one by one, individuals have found and followed the sometimes obvious and sometimes faint pathways to a point from which it is possible to take a larger view.

During the past relatively short span of 4,000 to 5,000 years there have evolved among us individuals who somehow have remembered the direct connection that exists between Humanity and the Creator. These individuals have taken it upon themselves to communicate to others how that remembrance came to be. From this process certain guidelines have come down to us in a number of different spiritual disciplines or religions, which were presented in forms and language appropriate to the cultures and understanding of the time. Spanning outward from these individuals, there seems to have been an impulse of light and energy which transformed the world of their time and thereafter.

These pulsings of light and energy resulted in the formation of civilizations which carried forward the transformation until those forms became solid and thus were subject to erosion. During the periods of the light itself and the formation phases of the civilizations, many individuals experienced personal transformation, and thus their families, their local communities, and their nations took on some of the qualities of the enlightenment and for a time thrived and even flourished.

During the period beginning with the early solidifying of the last light impulse and the dawning of this new impulse which is now making itself known, the possibilities for personal enlightenment have been extremely limited. These between-light periods are periods of savagery, of dominance and submission, of wars of conquest where only the tyrannies of gangdom seemed viable. In such times arts, philosophy and simple human good will have all but disappeared or have manifested privately or in small groups and families, essentially underground.

I say we are now in a period where the last light pulse has solidified and where gangdom has held sway over masses of humanity. We are also in a period of the new light dawning. In fact, it seems to many of us that there are two different worlds in which we now operate. To be sure, gangdom in its many forms still seems to dominate in our city streets, in our armed nations, in our adversarial politics, in our appetites for din, drugs, distractions and our addiction to violence. This addiction is rooted solidly in twin myths: one, that there is not enough to go around and two, that violence works to achieve survival in a dangerous world. Thus we have the paradigm of gangdom, with its perpetual trade-off of eyes and teeth, conqueror and conquered. We have as well the obscene imbalance whereby the few victors consume to satiety the world's supply of fuel, food, clothing and shelter while allowing bare survival supply to the majority of humanity.

But witness the collapse of gangdom in places where it had held rigid and bloody control for decades in parts of Eastern Europe, Africa, South and Central America and Asia. The last tyrants of humanity, throwbacks to earlier times, are one by one beginning to totter off into history or are being dispersed in murky clusters by the new light that is dawning. However, we should know by now that wherever this dispersal is caused by rebellion or invasion, tyranny in altered forms will return again and again.

And still, even now, individuals and families divided by class, gender and other contrived differences are wallowing in the brutality of racism and ethnic violence, being hateful, resentful, isolated and dangerous. And others are becoming locked in the stance of rebellion just when the forms of darkness against which they protest and rebel are shown to be nothing in the dawning of the light, leaving them to stew in their rebelliousness, or to turn themselves and become the light.

    We, Humanity, in growing numbers are learning of our power to create, and many people of all ages and cultural backgrounds are experiencing an urgency to be and see, create and become what is beautiful, elegant and noble. This is simply a function of who we are, sibling children of God, who are beginning to remember.

Children of Light

Each of us is a composite being. We are at once child of God/spirit/human being operating in a Homo sapiens body. In spirit, we and our children are siblings. As composite creatures we have roles to play and our children have roles to play. We who operate as adults have the task of caring for, protecting and training the infants, children, and adolescents until they are mature enough to operate autonomously as contributing members of the human family.

The maturity required to operate autonomously does not manifest automatically as a function of chronological aging. Chronological "maturity," undirected, unguided, and uncivilized, often results in another bully, gangster or warlord, or the inverse images of these, their toadies and minions still to be seen all a-row, "secure" in their obeisance to the chief. But there are also those born into social and economic poverty, often brutalised and deprived of training or encouragement, who display an autonomous character and creative prominence seemingly from birth. With these it is as though they arrived trained and ready to contribute from day one. Even they require the presence of adults who are there to teach them the languages and methods of operation in the culture in which which they are born.

Ideally this training process takes place as a cooperative venture, a conscious collaboration of the human beings involved, aligned and operating as one or more committed adults and one or more infants becoming adult in their care. These human beings, in spirit, are siblings. The Homo sapiens are adult and child.

These marvelous, aligned human beings, given the knowledge that can be acquired from our accumulated wisdom, can bring into being by love, training and example a remarkably efficient, useful, love-giving and joyful composite being in whom all will be most pleased.

In this time of the new dawning of the light such beings are going to have the opportunity to participate in a miraculous time in the story of mankind. Despite appearances to the contrary, this is a marvelous time to be born into the world, and realization of this is showing up even now among many of our young. Many of our spiritual siblings have already arrived and many more are knocking at the door. They will need love, protection and wise counsel and training. Ready or not, it is up to us to fill that need.

Each One of Us Makes a Difference

It is often said, "Well, a man's got to be someplace." That happens to define quite well an operational rule for a human being operating a Homo sapiens on the planet Earth. A corollary to that rule is that where one is operating, and with whom, is not an accident. This is an assertion that I make. Logic and sorted and filtered data could be assembled for or against the veracity of that assertion. For present purposes I propose posing it as a question and holding it open as one lives one's life. It has been my experience that doing so provides an increasing certainty that it is so. One is where one is, and with whom, and there are no accidents.

Now add that what one is experiencing is the direct result of causes one has set in motion as human being with or without Homo sapiens-in-tow. Add further that the initiation of those causes takes place in the context of the conversation being participated in by that individual human being and by all Humanity.

Among the data that has come my way is this: we humans, billions of us, in or out of incarnation, were created at the same moment by God. We are, now and always, as we were created, the living image and extension of the Creator. We, human being, are therefore sibling children of God. Now, that is either a living fact, or it is not. Whether or not that is a fact, it can be used as an operating proposition. Basically that proposition is the basis for the flourishing of human life on this planet, and I am using it as the premise which, if operational in human sub-groups, renders them workable and successful groups.

A contrary proposition can also be operational. All forms of human cruelty, all forms of tyranny, all organizations designed to stifle the life and creativity and possibility of joy for human beings, come forth from the operating proposition that each human being is essentially separate and alone and therefore fearful and dangerous, each to each. The presence of that operating premise essentially guarantees that at some point the human sub-group will break down and tear itself apart. That goes for friendships, marriages, work groups, sports teams, church bodies, tavern regulars, armed forces, religions, nations, federations, alliances—any human endeavor involving two or more gathered in the name of any goal or purpose, be it monstrous, mundane or magnificent. Our human sub-groups flourish or self-destruct by virtue of which of these propositions is operational. Do we see ourselves as sibling children of the same God? Or, do we consider ourselves as separate from creation and from one another and therefore see our brother and sister humans as rivals and always potentially dangerous to our separate and fearful selves?

I propose that where one or more participants in any group endeavor are willing to hold open to the proposition that he/she and every other one is, indeed, a sibling child of God, that group has the possibility of transcending breakdown and overcoming the backflow of ego fear and attack. I say again, any one can bring that to any group situation and thus bring forward as a stable operating datum that two or more gathered as sibling children of their creator have the power of co-creation with that Creator. Such a result requires only declared acknowledgement and not effort or struggle.

On the Edge of Formlessness

This is an image, a perception of what I think is so out there. Each of us is a created being, discrete and yet one with each other and creation and the Creator. We have our being on the edge of formlessness and all forms come forth from here. We are ideas of the Creator. Before the form is, I am: an idea. When I think a thing, it forms. When you see it and acknowledge it you create it too. Thus we are co-creators of our world.

So this is what is happening now, at this right now moment, as these words are being formed and placed on my computer screen. Words are primal forms in the universe of form. Words are symbols and what comes forth from our words are constructs; illusions, games. Words generate images which, in turn, become interrelated each to each. We are created in the image of the Creator. And we live and breathe and have our being in that Image. In that Image we have been given, among other attributes, the attribute of creativity. Here on the edges of formlessness we can choose to make forms of our own choices as discrete individuals, or, we can choose to co-create with the Creator. The choice to create "on our own," sets up these weird and wonderful lifetimes we so "enjoy" and which we think we are in danger, always, of "losing." I consider it possible that our choice to co-create with the Creator brings with it a high potential of peace and even joy.

The great civilizations of man were times of stability and relative peacefulness which are characteristic of how it is on the edges of formlessness. Those among us who perceive ourselves as trapped in back alleyways of crumbling cities tend to be less than civilized, too often mean and suspicious, despite the fact that we are always one instant's choice away from the source of civilization, the edges of formlessness.

Bach conceived his music from the edges of formlessness. He dedicated each composition, we are told, to the glory of God. I translate that to mean that Bach operated as co-creator, here on the edges of formlessness. Thus the power and vitality and the joy of his music. Even now, I acknowledge that the source of all knowledge can be contacted by each of us here on the edges of formlessness. I propose that it is possible for each or any of us to spend lifetimes rattling around (I get the image of rats and alley cats) among the forms we have made as individuals and families and clans and gangs and nations. And no matter how involved we are in the games we have made, no matter how "survival" we think our roles to be, always we are here on the edges of formlessness—at peace and in joy. Of this we can be reminded. Art, literature, music, dance, the theater, poetry and the sacred writings from the dawns of civilizations are the reminders to those who are listening, that we, Humanity, are in the Image of the Creator and do have our being, now, on the edges of formlessness. We always have the choice, now, to be at peace as co-creators or continue to rattle around among the clutter and trash of our own making.

I say that the "good food" for the minds and hearts of our young must be provided, as reminders of our Humanity. In the alleyways among the garbage cans we are, as "ET," very much wanting to go home. Our children, not yet so involved in the struggles of cats and rats, are much more aware of this. They are much more remindable. For a time. Thus the importance of books and all the arts.

Bach co-created among the precisions of fugue and toccata, among the disciplines of instrument and voice. These forms he used as does the sculptor the clay or the granite. These forms were put to use to the glory of the Creator. It seems to me very clear right now that each and any of us can do that, no matter what the forms are that we are now attending to.

So It's Not Christmas

Just because it isn't Christmas doesn't mean that we aren't alive and well and connected to you. We are, after all, forever friends.

So I thought I would write something to affirm and confirm and renew that connection. Writing is my way of actualizing what I, at this very moment, sense to be what is so. When I write this way I really never know at the first word what will unfold from the words that follow. I do imagine words to be living things, charged and breathing and lighted. I choose to be responsible for those I send forth and I reserve the right to contradict them at some later moment and context when other words are closer to what, for me, is so. You have the right to find that inconsistent and unacceptable, or with me, you may consider it my work in progress.

I do not know, as truth, what I am about to say. I see this kind of discourse as though I were working on a canvas or a sculpture. It takes form more often than not as a surprise, and often I am willing to risk a "yes" or a "that sounds to be right-on" when this day's work gets said and done.

Now hear this. We, Humanity, evolve "outward" from Center, now and forever, and impinge on and dance with matter, energy, space and time as co-creators, from that Center, of cosmos amid chaos. We seek then to share universes in the words we must speak and the songs we must sing. And we dance. We do! We act in great dramas down here in the slowness of time, sometimes forgetting that we are actors and dancers and poets and singers of songs. We forget, or deny it. And forgetting, we are left with tuning our perceptors to the illusion that the play is what is so. And in the thrall of the play we learn how to struggle, suffer and then seem to die. A few times in a given life span one or another of us gets an inkling, a sense that we are involved in some kind of cosmic joke. Perhaps this is because when we look back in time we often see that our life is an evolving wholeness, lived separately, day to day, or that our life experience has a logic to it, and even a purpose. And then we wonder how this is so.

Down through history there have been the few, less cursed than we with forgetfulness—artists, scientists, philosophers—who knew and spoke and formed the music and knowledge born of their vision. And they passed their vision on so that, thank God, there are people, even statesmen, who show up, often just in time, who are willing to consider other possibilities than just more of the same.

For instance, there is Vaclav Havel, playwright and president, alive and well and living in our own time, who says:

> *The question is…whether we shall, by whatever means, succeed in reconstituting the natural world as the true terrain of politics; in rehabilitating the personal experience of human beings as the initial measure of things; in placing morality above politics and responsibility above our desires; in making human community meaningful; in returning content to human speaking; in reconstituting, as the focus of all social action, the autonomous, integral and dignified human "I," responsible for ourselves because we are bound to something higher, and capable of sacrificing something, in extreme cases everything…for the sake of that which gives life meaning.*

There is Vaclav Havel and, as a function of his presence, there are others who will make themselves known as one, remembering, turns up the light for another to remember, thus passing it on. For certain this is a time for us as individuals to do The Work, the daily work of re-awakening, of remembering. It is now our privilege to make contact from our autonomous centers to the Center from which we evolved and thus give legitimacy and power to what has been muttering and flashing just over the horizon like an approaching prairie thunderstorm. There is an evolving world consciousness, a shift of paradigm from nation view to global view, there is! Just now that shift resides within individuals scattered in increasing number throughout this lovely small planet. Their very presence is causing, no, not causing, signaling the end to what I say are the last angry nationalistic and racist reactions, the cruelty of which we are witnessing world wide. Perhaps it is now, or soon to be, another manifesto time. Perhaps now it is time for another declaration with the awakening and energizing power of our Declaration of Independence.

Perhaps, even now new groups of founding fathers and mothers are gathering in coffee shops, libraries, living rooms and in committees of correspondence creating the words that will light the future for global brotherhood in a context of racial, ethnic and philosophic diversity, a world that works for everybody, with no one left out.

So It's Not Christmas

I would share with you that I simply do not buy into what's on the surface right now. When I am tempted, as I often am, to fret, rave and march, I am cautioned to pause, to hold, to look deeply, to listen within. And in those quiet moments, from that listening, it seems appropriate to acknowledge and align with a dream whose time has come.

Alan AtKisson of the Context Institute of Seattle, Washington, calls it "Earth's dream, the image of a planet exuberantly alive and its most potent and dangerous creatures—human beings—living together in creative peace." AtKisson says further, "Millions of people, more and more every day, are having this dream. It is a dream of hope, of life, of a meaningful future. More accurately, this dream is having us. We have no choice but to dream it, to speak it—to make it real."

Yes! With that dream I sense an urgency to invest my joy, to **en**-joy that dream, to let it go forth as a smile goes forth, including all, on out unto the farthest galaxy. And in the doing it becomes quite clear, that, in a little while, inevitable as Spring.........it will be done.

War No More

It takes a while for an idea to dawn. Idea may be too active a word. What I would speak of here is as yet unspeakable, pre-verbal. It is more question than answer.

We Americans have, for several generations, come to expect to be able to set up a lifetime of reasonable comfort and stability and to witness and partake of the joys and surprises of several generations coming in to maturity. We called this the American Dream. Some of us came to know it as personal reality. Out of this came the almost certainty, for many, that life was somehow under our control. In order to enjoy this "certainty" it was only necessary to believe that somehow we American humans were special humans and that, unlike most others, we deserved our peace and stability. We had earned it, you see, by being special.

True, there were the times of trouble and the wars: World War I, the Great Depression, World War II, the Korean Police Action, Viet Nam and the constant involvement of some people somewhere in civil wars, revolutionary wars and national wars of "liberation." On and on they go, constant since the "successful" conclusion of the war to end all war, in 1918. Life was under our control, you could say, except for those who were involved in one or another of these disasters. Most human beings in this time knew disaster was possible but it was almost always something that happened to others, in another place and time. Superstition, nationalism, magic incantations such as "A strong defense is our only security" or "We will have peace even if we have to go to war for it"—or lines drawn in sand and chips placed on shoulders amid much macho muttering—have increasingly made it apparent that prepared and armed or not, this "war thing" is not under our control. And so we continue to bleed our economies dry to be able to "win" battles. We cheer our leaders who snarl about our many enemies, "Bring them on!" This, in the relative safety of an adoring citizenry.

We have been living out our lives, generation to generation, in the thrall of a myth that war—force—is a legitimate exercise of our creative power as human beings. We have been stuck with the belief system that says that winning by the use of force is the only alternative to losing to a superior force.

Paradigm is the current word for such a belief system, having taken over from other words such as myth, prejudice, ongoing world conversation. A paradigm as I use the word here is the context in which we perceive what is going on in the world. It is what we as human beings believe without question about ourselves and about other human beings. Paradigm changes occur ever so slowly. Fads such as peace movements change rapidly once it is claimed (with or without evidence) that the enemy is bestial, kills babies and rapes women—behaviors that no one on "our side" would even think of doing. Paradigms are more all-encompassing belief systems, less provincial. A paradigm-sized belief system is the one that our warhawk leaders share with our warhawk-led "enemy" nations and our warhawk-led allied nations. The warhawk paradigm has dominated the consciousness of mankind for God knows how long; certainly it was dominant among the peoples of the Old Testament. Certainly it is still rare to find a brother human being who is willing to grant a place in the sun to every other human being.

Yes, it does take a while for an idea to dawn. It takes even longer for a paradigm to set below the horizons of history. Actually the old paradigm sets only with the dawn of the new one, much as the leaves of the red oak tree let go finally only as the buds of Spring begin to open.

I said that this paradigm shift from warhawk consciousness to that which is budding even now, is still pre-verbal, spoken more in silence than in word form. But these few words are not alone. There are others speaking out, others in the number of hundreds of thousands. We speak now universally in poem and song, and we dream of the way it is to be when we study war no more.

Beachhead

Human being, with Homo sapiens in tow, inches forward now all along the frontier where a beachhead is expanding away from the adversarial swamps. We are still very close to the swamp and the miasma burping forth therefrom is at times nearly overwhelming. We daily, even hourly, must deal with adversarial gasses coming forth from one or another of us still oozing from the swamps.

Here we are. We are human beings who have declared for the possibility it is to be human. Instead of doing angry combat with specters we no longer energize, we are learning to create new space and enlarge the beachhead. Each moment we do that, moves us forward. That is so, and we come to know that it is so.

Here and there one of us must deal with another one wrestling and agitated, involved again in spectral thrall in one form or another—angry, accusing, heading again toward the swamp. Gassed these are, from some swamp bubble burping. What do we do for these? Try to stop them? Or, do we get out of their way? What do you do when someone on the beachhead declares that you are the enemy?

It is good and useful to recognize that what you are observing here is Homo sapiens behavior under the thrall of a separated self, an ego. If you intend to be useful to your fellow human being here, and that is inevitable unless you too are becoming enthralled, you must look past the Homo sapiens, the behavior, and acknowledge the fellow human, silently being there.

Engage with the human being then—silently or in vocal conversation. Remind him that he has achieved the beachhead and that he doesn't have to go back into the swamp. Remind him that all he is experiencing is a temporary breakdown. Remind him that his choice, right now, can be for miracles. His choice can be "yes"—toward life. Do that now and do nothing else. Proceed then on your journey. Know that by your quick action, all the help that he is able to accept is with him.

Beachhead

By what authority do I make such a promise? As Tevya says in *Fiddler on the Roof*, "Well, I'll tell you......I don't know."

First, it's not my promise, and I am persuaded by personal experience that the promise is valid. Please note that I am addressing this to those who, with me, have recently reached the beachhead, who have just recently crawled out of the reactive soup, those who now realize the futility of the enemy game. I am conversing with your ego/Homo sapiens, and mine. This conversation is by way of a reminder that we are, first, human being. I am dealing with the reality that reactive patterns can again become operative when we become, (and we do) temporarily forgetful that we are first, human being.

Reactive patterns begin to lose their power when we, human being, choose to discard the presumptive little ego and instead, choose miracles, which is the choice by which we achieved the beachhead. The only power patterns have comes from the energy of our own misdirection of attention. We have the moment by moment choice to activate the old patterns, or to choose miracles. We all experience the reactivation of old patterns. We all experience flare ups and upsets. Our first concern in these early days is to be aware of these events as they come up, and then to let them be. Nod to them, say "hello." Someone said, "I just thank them for sharing, and then I choose miracles." Unfed by our attention and our dramatizations, these patterns literally wear out. They become inoperable. Their only source of power is our own attention, our own misdirected attention. Every time they gain our attention they are revived a bit. Every time we choose not to attend to them though they seem so logical and useful, so necessary for survival, we render them less; finally they are as useless as last year's leaves. More useless, for they don't even make mulch.

The March storm has passed. The wind has subsided. The last deep winter cold has moved in. The song birds must wait a while, south of us. As in the fall when we wait as the winter locks in, as the winter silence approaches, now we wait as the winter silence reasserts itself this one more time. But there are signs. There is stirring. Last week we first saw a lone pair of geese heading north, and later in the week a gaggle of ten more, sketching and erasing their lines across the sky. The leaves which the red oak cling to all winter though they are lifeless and useless to the tree, these brown ghosts of oak leaves are being discarded now. They have been rattling across the snow crust for several days now, stacking up here and there, released at last. Ready to serve their last service, mulch for the new growth coming.

By what authority do I promise this new spring coming? Please, I just said it is not my promise and I am persuaded by personal experience that winter drops away. Spring comes at last. Honest!

Can We?
Political Campaign 1992

The political conventions are now underway. As I participate in this activity via the media, I hear Rodney King (the man recently beaten severely by Los Angeles police) say, so plaintively, "Can we all get along?"

Upon hearing this, I answer, "Yes, but not this political, adversarial way." Then I consider the opposing candidates and their campaigns as they are taking shape. It is clear that each campaign has, high on its agenda, the invalidation and the condemnation of the other. Quite aside from the curious fact that we use the military word "campaign" for all of this, this intention to invalidate the other is parallel to the intentions of armies doing battle. Good will is not involved. Each assumes harmfulness to be the intention of the other. In 1988 the presidential campaign got under way with the derisive "Where was George" speech of then-Governor Ann Richards of Texas. The subsequent "victor," George Bush, used fear images, ridicule and flag waving like the weaponry he later turned loose in Panama and Desert Storm. At that time, it was clear to many that this method of carrying on politically was and is harmful. Harmful to the "vanquished," harmful to the "victors" and harmful to our human environment since it practically guarantees an uncooperative and hostile atmosphere for the duration of the "victors" time in office.

To all of this I say, "There must be a better way."

Consider this. The worldwide environment which we humans have collectively caused to be, clearly requires some tender loving care if we are to enjoy or even survive our transition into the twenty-first century. Intelligent and thoughtful people capable of tender loving thinking will be required at all levels of society to make the world work with any kind of peacefulness and harmony. Failure to include all humanity in the effort will deprive it of the necessary aligned creative energy.

I say that the present method of attack/defend politics makes such an alignment of creative energy practically impossible and therefore any real solutions to problems highly unlikely. I want to make it clear that this dire conclusion is related to the methods we have traditionally used to carry out our political process. Parties who live by attack/defend will be rendered ineffective by attack/defend. It's as simple as that. Someone recently pointed out that agreement is less important than respect, for with respect agreement may one day occur, but without it agreement is impossible. That to me effectively summarizes the disaster potential should we continue to operate politically as we have been doing.

Can we all get along? Can we evolve a civilized, peaceful method of airing problems and finding solutions that invites the cooperative gathering of the creative energies of all? Can the "buck" of attack/defend stop at last, here in this political process now underway?

I do not pretend to have the answer as to how this could be brought about but I ask of all the parties concerned that they recognize how necessary it is for good will and mutual respect to be in place when the vote is in and all the seats of government are filled for the next period.

I know that there are voices which would say that respect must be earned. But the simple truth is that respect can only be given. Respect, as I use it here, means simply that one party grant to the other party, candidate or person the right to be alive in the world. Esteem, deference, veneration, loving one's neighbor as oneself, these are respect written large. These are wonderful gifts to give another, but the respect I refer to is simply that of granting to another being the right to be. This is an inner act whereby one chooses to accept rather than deny the presence in the world of any other being. Accepted or denied, it is a wonderful fact that all beings exist now and forever more. When one of us neglects to grant beingness to another, the result is to becloud our own perception of what is so.

In the space occupied by such respect, attack/defend no longer can function. When mutual respect is there, we can all get along. As I see it, respect or attack/defend is a choice each has the privilege and the opportunity to make. Try it out on the most snarly, hateful, contentious person you can think of, and silently say, "(His or her name), I grant you the right to be here on the planet with me."

When you do this, instead of avoiding the person or denying his or her presence, we include him or her within our physical, emotional and spiritual environment. Do that, and a very real wall comes tumbling down—and we create an opportunity to listen to and hear another human being, which is the necessary first step to a positive answer to "Can we all get along?"

Declaration of Intent

When I embarked upon this voyage, the thought did not occur that the voyage would end. That thought now occurs with increasing frequency. The exact time of arrival is not clear to me. What is clear is what I would intend and declare before I disembark:

1. To live in good health, strength and vitality up to my committed time for transition. My transition to be accomplished quietly and in joy for what lies ahead, and absolutely minimal mess and fuss for family and friends. Continue to do The Work, to get more certain and closer to the only power in the universe, God. To pass that on as certainty, so that others come to certainty too, and they pass it on. To be guiltless, forgiven. To bless all I have touched in this life that they be guiltless, forgiven, too. To become increasingly skilled in writing what is so for me, in poems, essays, letters, mutterings. That they be read and used as means of passing along the certainty of our creative power as human being. That the spiritual fact of abundance continue to manifest as affluence in our lives, as plenty and plenty for all.

2. To come forth from my shell in my relationship to my spiritual partner, to really be open to the joy she truly is. To accept the empowerment of her love and support by letting it light up both our lives, that we truly be one in spirit. That this light then shine forth in the lives of Leesa and Nancy and Stephen and the grandchildren, that they, in turn, pass it on, pass it on. That the light enlighten the lives of our new daughter, Megumi, and Janette's violin students and her nephew and nieces, and their parents, that they in turn pass it on, pass it on.

3. To function in each chosen group endeavor in such a way that the purposes being served by the group are enhanced by our participation, that miracles be shared by all concerned. That this activity expand into art and creativity

as a means of transformation, as a way of life. That we open up so that we can more effectively facilitate harmony in the personal relationships in each group in which we function.

4. It is time for sanity to manifest in every corner of the planet. In place of ethnic savagery, ethnic celebration. Instead of the enemy game, human creativity devoted to making the world work for everyone, with no one left out. We now finish our struggle to conquer others, to use our creative power to dominate others. Instead we co-operate on this planet and give space and time and ear to each individual, to each ethnic group, each nation and race and people to fully realize just how magnificent mankind is, just how magnificent each human individual is.

The arts have always reminded us of this down through the ages. The higher the civilization the more advanced and uplifting have the arts and the artists been. Now life itself will become the art work, and the light hinted at in the art work of all the masters known and obscure, will shine forth through individuals and through each individual, bringing such light forth that the miracles previously thought necessary to bring the world to its true destiny will manifest everywhere and be considered, as they are, natural.

We see no reason for this present human struggle to continue. We have all learned the harm we can do, not one of us has not harmed others. We have experienced the cost. It is time now to drop our self-generated denial of our power and accept the fact that we have created what we are experiencing, each and every one of us.

The surf is up. The light is lit. Time now to go for it.

Here We Are

The first few years of the 21st Century have passed. I have often said that I wanted to be (actually, I planned to be) "here" at the turn of the century. And "here" I am.

"Here"—a place in space and time, geographical on the surface of the planet Earth, chronological in relation to the spinning of the planet around the sun, astronomical in relation to the billions of satellites, planets, star systems, novas, black holes, galaxies that make up the "big bang." Wheee! "Look, Mom! Look at me!" When I reach out to comprehend it, for a moment I do not breathe and I simply spin on out, out to the edge of it all. When I resume breathing, I am "here." Now. As always.

Right now I am aware that this "here" is entirely other than rocks and bodies flying away from each other in an eternal explosion of matter, energy, space and time. From a point smaller than this period "." (actually smaller than that—infinitesimal, smaller than zero!) has come this, this all-that-there-is. And it is still coming. And going! And I am part of it as are you and each and every one of us. And we are here still within and part of that which is smaller than zero.

"Who says?" you ask.

Well for starters, I say it. I hazard it. It is showing up as I clatter on this keyboard. But more. The word shape of it has been formed by prophets and seers and saints and masters from the time of the oldest written records presently available. Formed also by poets and singers right up to the present day. From the proud men of modern science have come the means of perception, the logic and mathematics that now underwrites this awesome reality. Long imagined and divined, faith revealed, now it is possible to have a tenuous grasp on that which is so. Or is it?

Well, there are words. Words about it. But what do I know? I have inklings that glitter in words and colors and lights and tones and chords. I am "here." That, I know. I sense, I project, I declare I have always been here. Now. Here now as the centuries and millennia turned and spiraled in the bang, "I" and "here" are entirely other than all that comprises matter, energy, space and time. I am being. Here. Now. Forever. I would collapse the actuality of this to conform to words. Perhaps a silent song or the tiniest sharpest clearest "ping" or "bong" so penetrating and profound as to silence all else.

"Here" I am, I say. And "here" are you.

"Here" becomes "I am." Only words. I say "love." I say your name. I embrace silence, take it in. I absorb the music of silence, the beat of it, that…………I am. Holy. Aaauuum. Center. No thing.

I want to say it. I would give birth to a word…………..No word yet, but this glitter of connection that comprises all being, thee and me. All that lives, all, thee, me, bang and ping and bong.

Oh, what a moment this is! This right-now moment of May 2003.

The Problem of Certainty

The Curse

Much of the struggle and strife going on in the world springs from our human proneness to create "safe harbors" of belief where we can seem to be secure behind breakwaters of false certainty.

It is legitimate to seek to know what is actually so regarding God, man and the universes. The plate of possibilities is full. Perhaps it is more accurate to say that the array of possibilities is in storage bins of gradient probability from, say, highly improbable (nothing thinkable being impossible) constructs about the nature of God, man and the universes, to highly probable constructs by the trusted operation of which we more or less successfully live out our lives. From near impossibility to realities just this side of certainty, so goes this gradient of what may be so. Seen this way the array of bins of possibility from possible through probable would always be other than what is actually so. It is this consideration that is on my agenda at this time. What is actually so, for me, is more often than not, not so for any other person, therefore, there are either two or more actualities that differ, or, they are not actualities at all. If not actualities, then we are dealing with beliefs or opinions, no matter how certain we are as individuals, of what is actually so. All beliefs and opinions therefore can best be considered as constructs of possibility, not what is actually so.

I propose that the divisive struggles going on between ethnic groups and among true believers, and hate engendering arguments such as when does a fetus become human, are understandable in the context of our unwillingness to operate in a world of infinite possibilities, rather than one of declared certainties. It seems to me that the hatefulness and bitterness comes up, often to the point where murder has been "justified," because it is too fear engendering for one to hold as only a possibility that which one has, in the past, held to be certain. It seems that for some there cannot be found a common ground, shared with others, which accommodates more than one certainty. And yet, for me, there is precious little, if anything, of which I am certain. At least little comes to mind of a magnitude for which I would be willing to become hateful. And yet I sometimes come close to condemnation (a form of hate) in relation to those who would bully and even kill others to promote their certainties.

While I do find homicidally intolerant people just barely tolerable, I would hardly feel justified in brutalizing them or shelling their towns and villages or making their lives all but barely livable. In fact, it seems to me that violent confrontations of those who are certain put people into a region of consciousness where that which seems certain is clutched, hung on to and defended even unto death. What has come to mind as I wrote the above is this. Let me state what is here in concept form.

- Beliefs and opinions which we call certainties are mental constructs, graven images, idols, icons which we create ourselves or adopt from others' creations. Some of these have formed for us "with our mother's milk." They derive from the culture in which we are born and become "civilized." If we find that these certainties "work" for us, they become more and more real, more solid and are thus passed on to following generations.

- A common denominator of such certainties is that we experience them as having power coming from elsewhere. However, they derive power from the assignment and agreement of each of us. Because we miss this vital reality, certainty becomes to us something beyond our control—legitimized by Authority. We now have reached a condition of dependency on the existence of a "higher" power outside of ourselves.

Now, when we are confronted by others whose certainties are to them and us (note the point of agreement) equal and opposite, we are face to face with the dilemma which empowers the racial, ethnic, tribal, religious, economic and territorial slaughter erupting all over this lovely small planet. We find the presence of an equal and opposite certainty intolerable. To even consider one or the other as possible rather than certain throws us into uncertainty and calls into question the Authority to which we have assigned the responsibility for our safety and survival. Thus comes fear riding forth on the horses of hatred.

Notice that this process of giving thought to a picture of what is wrong and how wrongness develops, does little to bring forth a way to go that brings peace and happiness to the scene. It is my thought that peace and happiness cannot come forth from beliefs and certainties which are derived from Authority. By our mistaken empowerment as certainties of this or that selection of images and abstractions of our culture, we create the killing grounds of our time and place. By our self-righteousness and our condemnation of others who do not conform to our certainties, we create the insanities of Rwanda and Bosnia, of Haiti and Desert Storm. And not just insanity out there and far away. We all are dealing with such insanities as chemical addiction and our addiction to violence in our homes and in our neighborhoods. We all are involved in condemnation in one form or another and are thus eroding in our very souls our ability to enjoy life and each other. We seem to be less and less inclined to express good will and participate joyfully in the human comedy. Yes, by our own misdirected creative energy we have created the specters by which we are cursed. And yet it is possible to use this same creative energy with which we are endowed to do other than create these cursing and cursed specters.

The Blessing

I would put forward—not as certainty but as possibility, as in simply "try this on to see how it will work"—the following:

- Happy people would have other people be happy, not as a prerequisite to their own happiness, but because there is a reciprocity of happiness which is exponential; it spirals out to include others more and more.

- Happiness is accessible to everyone but there is little training in how it can be experienced. Some things about the experience of happiness are known well enough to be replicated in the living of life itself. Bookstores display titles a-plenty which contain many technologies for the achievement of happiness, enough for anyone to find his own way. Recently I found a joy of a volume, entitled *Excuse Me, Your Life Is Waiting*, by Lynn Grabhorn.

- Happiness is the result of our own creation. Happiness cannot be caused for us by anyone or anything. We can cause happiness in ourselves by attending to beautiful forms and sounds and aromas and silences and yes, by extending our appreciation and admiration outward to include others and eventually all others. We can cause happiness in ourselves by creative living, by performance of beauty as artist and performer and thus extend our happiness, again, spiraling outward, more and more inclusively.

- Happiness, or at least humor and laughter, can be created in any context. Witness the jokes and laughter that some bring forth in the face of the grimmest misfortune. For the moment, in the presence of humor, the dire crisis is seen as other, by those who are laughing. Such transcendent moments are not perceived by those attending to their own miseries nor by those extending sympathy, i.e., agreement with and empowerment of the misery of others.

- It is not possible to be immersed in the experience of happiness and to be fearful, or hateful or even careless of the survival of others. It is not possible to be happy and at the same time intolerant or condemning of others.

- Happy people exude a great energy that pours forth from the very center of themselves. It is this seemingly boundless energy which en-joys, brings joy to, themselves first, and then the world around them. Of this only those who experience it can be certain. Those who think all energy comes from outside themselves cannot know happiness nor joy and are often found among those who believe that happiness is a form of evil.

It is the same energy by which we create, in the living of our moment-to-moment lives, the curses and the blessings of our time and place.

Of that idea, that possibility, I am tempted to say I am certain.

Declaration for Humanity

The world I am active in and share with neighbors, co-workers and family expands outward through woodlands, farms and towns, and spaceward and Earth's core-ward. It includes satellites in space and galaxies and the seething center of the planet. It includes a very satisfactory physical universe that works. It includes Kabul and Baghdad, Belfast and Jerusalem, New York City and Washington D.C. And all the centers of turbulence where things do not appear to work very well at all.

These centers of turbulence go on and on, replicating like some insane spreadsheet gone out of control. On the surface it sometimes seems that the adversarial and ideological specters overshadow these centers so completely as to prevent any hope that they will come to a higher balance. All over this beautiful little ample planet, babies are coming in to find themselves caught in ideological netting, and so ensnared are they, it is more than likely that most will become the new generation of adversaries.

And yet, even in those expanding centers of turbulence, there are families, co-workers and neighbors, probably a majority even now, who maintain the connections that are what it means to be human.

Everything about the planet itself, and the space it is in, still works; and yet increasingly, in just this last century, some ego/Homo sapiens are becoming so self-destructive that it sometimes seems that even the planet itself is in jeopardy.

I say that no good can come from attending to the centers of turbulence and the perpetrators therein. I say much more good can come from attending to the individuals, neighbors, co-workers and friends who are not destroyers—who are being from their humanity. I say that in human history there have always been those, usually just barely enough, who keep alive the human possibility of co-operating in the balancing manner of the planet and the universe as a whole.

Therefore: it is time to declare from my self, with my family, with my neighbors, with my co-workers and all the clusters of us around the planet everywhere, it is time to declare for what the possibilities are in being who we really are as human being. This is not a declaration of war. This is not advocacy of political action. This is the call to be who we really are. A shift is taking place—one by one by one—(the only way it can). A light exists which is increasingly perceivable. It cannot be doused. It can only expand and extend one-by-one-by-one through neighbors and friends and co-workers. The light, this shift toward who we are, comes not from outside us but from us. From our present level of consciousness it does not appear to exist full blown to be partaken of. It must be built in the manner of a conversation or a work of art. It begins right now with me, with my family, neighbors, friends, co-workers.

And so I begin in these promises: I will henceforth be alert to the inner conversation, the noises formed by the invisible ego, i, that little i. When that little one is evident, I will shift my attention out to those with whom I am in conversation and action. I will shut that little ego down as often as need be, and bridge across to my soul siblings, in discourse, and appropriately. I will learn from this and thus grow stronger. I promise to observe my words and the words I hear and the responses and reactions I experience in my discourse with my family, my neighbors, my co-workers and my friends. In and from that observation I will shift my speaking toward the end that what I speak out is an authentic reflection of what I am within. And when in this I experience the unfamiliar edge, my personal frontier, I'll continue on in faith, aligned with these promises and the possibility of human being.

The Democracy of Spirit

What a gift from the Universe it is to have this opportunity to share with others our versions of the way that it is and to enjoy how closely our versions often align. I maintain that all humanity is one being and therefore we share a common endowment of spirit. Thus we have the potential to participate in and enjoy the grand democracy of the spirit. As the poet Kahlil Gibran said, we were "born together and together we shall be forever more." I come from a view that humanity, all of us, are sibling children of a Creator who has endowed us with rights, responsibilities, and powers. As such, we experience an innate desire to make things work for the benefit of all who share life here on this lovely small planet.

And yet we have not come close to accomplishing that in all of the known history of our species. There have always been those few in every family, clan, nation and culture who claimed for themselves privileges and comforts beyond all need in contrast to the bare survival of all others. This disparity of conditions of living has always created tensions, stresses and strains so as to eventually tear apart the system that made the family, clan, nation or culture viable. It seems that systems that cause imbalance in the conditions of survival of all are doomed to fail. And the failure of these systems is experienced by all as tragedy and disaster. Could it be that the increasing tempo of disaster going on in our present world at the the beginning of the 21st century is signalling an imbalance of living conditions sufficient to tear apart the present way we all go about living our lives? Surely there is sufficient evidence to make such a question worthy of consideration.

For me, the most dynamic thought which is being stated all over the place, is, "There must be a better way."

Shades

During the past decade we have carried on a conversation regarding our views about the general condition of humanity in this world and this time. Often we speak of what could be and why it is not. In the latter category an idea is often brought forward that speaks of the existence of a hidden conspiracy involving a cabal of power intended people influencing our government policy and perhaps our world in general.

To conspire in our language means an intended, power-over-others alignment of two or more. So it is reasonable, I think, to say that when we direct our attention to the possibility of conspiracies of one kind or another we are looking through a "glass darkly." We take a dim (lightless?) view of life emerging around us.

When the conversation takes this focus of attention it results in a "darker" way of engagement. We judge, find wanting and condemn. Tiring of this onslaught on our creativity we subside into cynicism and thus neglect our true intention to add to "The Work" that I say we are here to do—to make the world work for everybody with no one left out. I for one am not willing for this darker way to divert us from making our spiritual contribution to humanity. For that is what we do with every word that proceedeth out of the mouth. Our frequent gathering creates a spiritual "power center" from which, more often than not, we come away pleased and thus recharged for engagement with the world. We have done "The Work" for this time and place. I say we can trust that others are in place to deal with whatever actual conspiracies exist.

We have been learning from so many sources—Werner Erhart's est, Deepak Chopra, A Course in Miracles, Neale Donald Walsch's *Conversations With God*, Marshall Vian Summers' Greater Community Spirituality—that we are the creators of our reality, individually and in the aggregate. Our personal lives and the world we live in are created and re-created in every moment of Now and form and form again as we individually and collectively choose. For me, this is no longer just a theory. It has become just a smidgen of doubt this side of certainty. That smidgen of doubt erupts most often when I allow the sometimes ugliness in the world to capture my attention. Then cynicism knocks and I must deny its entrance. When I refuse to be cynical, a conscious choice, well then, the light turns up, revealing an infinite array of possibilities, or sometimes, just quiet joy. I smile.

So, back to conspiracies and dark agendas of secret others. I propose that such gatherings exist in the imagination. It is in the imagination where we humans shape our realities about which we agree and disagree. That nation of images is our playground and our battlefield. And it is ours to do with as we will. As we freely will. Every moment of Now is just that. It simply is. At that moment we, in our imaginations, assign that moment and whatever we attend to, with whatever meaning we choose. In that process, on and on, all our heavens and hells emerge.

Just now I get that I should hush. That I be still and send this on to you, my friends. Let the conversation continue.

The Prevention and Creation of Supply

This time is one of those times when much......what?......energy, in a way—or better, food for the spirit—is coming in. There is energy in the form of information from books recently discovered. There is also energy in the form of an availability of fresh points from which to view old puzzles. Perhaps it is an influx of data from the higher self, our higher selves. Food for our thought. Supply of possibilities for consideration by mind and consciousness. For instance:

We live in a time when almost everyone alive on this small planet is dealing with problems of sustaining a supply of food, clothing and shelter in sufficient quantities and in such timely rhythms as to assure the survival of the human family unto future generations. I am here using the word supply to mean the availability of food, clothing, shelter and all the means and the symbols and efforts by which they are brought forth and exchanged. Supply, as I am speaking of it here, has to do with survival necessities.

No one is exempted from having to deal with supply as a problem. For millions in Africa, Asia and Central and South America the problem has become overwhelming and people are succumbing by the tens of thousands daily. For a few it may seem that the problem of supply never has existed. It is safe to say that for the majority of those in Europe, U.S. and Canada the problems of sustainable supply keeps us, as we perceive things, on an ongoing tightwire from which we can plunge at any moment. Homo sapiens, it seems, lives in an ongoing crisis of supply. It has been said, and I believe it, that for the past fifty or more years there has been no technical, logistical, agricultural, meteorological or even common sense cause for this seemingly perpetual crisis.

At any time in this past fifty years, by assigning ourselves, say, a twenty-year project to do so, we humans could have brought ourselves out of the crisis of supply at far less cost than we expended to land on the moon and probe the planets

The Prevention and Creation of Supply

and generate artificial crises of supply in Iraq and other horror spots we have caused to be around the world.

Assigning ourselves the task of accomplishing a worthy purpose is a function of mind and consciousness. Denying the existence of a perpetual crisis of supply, and therefore obscuring the marvelous possibilities there are to bring an end to it, is a function of mind and consciousness. Mind and consciousness individually and collectively generate in living forms that which we focus on. We all know that, of course. It seems that most of us still deny that we do.

And, one by one, there are those who acknowledge at last that we have this power. There have always been a few of these, perhaps just enough to keep humanity viable on this planet, but it seems that this influx of energy that I referred to above is increasing, is showing up in unexpected places. More and more people are operating on the assumption that human beings have creative power and that our power is used to create, for good or ill, the quality of life being experienced and the supply that becomes available.

So why do I find it appropriate to say this in the present time and format? Perhaps it's a product of this thought: Here we are defining, examining, pondering the power that we are as mind and consciousness, and that is good. It is good to understand what we are learning from our study. It is good, even necessary, to then ground it—to imagine what is yet to be as a product of the mind and consciousness work we are doing. No, I am not saying we now have to go forth and do something. I still say this conversation is a significant doing of something. I am saying what I perceive within me as a desire to accelerate this dawning of creative power that is one by one enlightening and energizing each of us. Creative power is a power sans arrogance, sans force, sans argument and persuasiveness. Silent. An engine of goodwill to all. Full with laughter and eyes flashing one-to-one in recognition and then acknowledgement. Do you get it? It's not an urge that we all agree on something and form ourselves into another political or ad hoc something or other. The world has had enough of that. We need to replenish our forests more than we need more organizations. (How's this for a slogan?—"When you feel the urge to change someone else, plant a tree instead.") I don't pretend to have made clear what I am sensing is alive in the world right now, this energy, these immense possibilities. I don't know! Here, you take it on from here. See what you can do with it.

The Gong

Each day, each moment, is an opportunity to fold one's awareness into the silence, to disappear into the void, to become at center, to breathe in rhythm with the universe. These opportunities are not things of time. They are an ongoing constant without beginning or end. I, this one alive in time, I intend to know this beyond the words, the use of which can erect a barrier to knowledge which holds me away from the breathing of the universe, until..........

"What was that?!"

All had heard it—a huge sound that rolled, intruded, reverberated, filled and vibrated among orchard slopes and vineyards along the great river valleys. Heard, too, in city canyons, in ships, in trains and traffic and jet planes crisscrossing seas and firmament. It was a sound that literally filled every empty space in mind and body and form and thought of every human every creature every plant and planet, every insect and tree, every sand grain, pebble and mountain. The deaf heard it, the blind, and infants on either side of first breath heard it. Heard, too, it was by gray, blue-veined, white-haired terminal ones just then teetering on the edges of their memories, no longer here at all but tethered still to pumps and tubes, and wheezing like Orcas moving slowly down the bay.

Oh, what a sound it was! That gong! The wholeness of the sound moved spherically from its center and source, wherever that was, or wasn't, and expanded and imploded at once—exploded and contracted so that not one quark or boson or electron or proton or gross molecule or atom was left not quivering. Huge and yet gentle. All that is and was and is yet to be absorbed and accepted and wondered at the sound and yet, all knew the beginning had come. At last, after all that had not really happened as humankind practiced co-creation, the beginning had come upon us all and the day was ours.

We had practiced enough.

Listen......................GONNNNG!

Regarding Words

Early on in Book 1 of Neale Donald Walsch's *Conversations With God*, God refers to "the unbelievable limitation of words." I got that words were not His favorite communication tool. He says that feeling is the language of the soul. Next in line for usefulness is thought, which transmits via images and pictures. And then He says that experience is the "grand communicator." I had never thought of that. Then He states that words are symbols of what is so, and words are not, themselves, that which is so. I had thought of that, or at least I had input that as information from books on semantics such as S. I. Hayakawa's *Language in Thought and Action*.

Among a group who have been reading and discussing the Conversations With God books, a few in the group were not comfortable with a scale that places words at the bottom of the scale of relative usefulness for purposes of communicating what is so. Personally, I stand with the idea that words do not and cannot take the place of feelings or experience or mental images. In the complicated process of communicating what is so, we often hear the phrase, "It goes without saying." When I step out my door and walk to where a large red oak tree stands, I have a choice to go there with my symbol reader on or I can shut that down and go there with all my 126 perceptors full on. When my symbol reader tells me "tree," I nod and say, "Yep, tree." And that suffices to register the fact that the tree is in its proper place. The word tree handles the transaction between tree and me and suffices to inform you that I have a tree in my yard and you acknowledge that as a high probability because your symbol tree responded to the word tree.

However, on another day I went forth to the tree fully alive and alert and awake in present time, and I had a whomping grand experience with that tree—actually with the livingness of that tree, livingness being the common denominator between me and tree.

Now there is no way that I could transmit to you the delicious experience of that moment by saying the word "tree." Actually the words "thank you" could better say it. Perhaps I could take you out to the tree and have you replicate what I did to have that experience, but that is what I think was meant by the difficulty of using words. I admit that Shakespeare and Martin Luther King and other master poets have come very close to the eternal reality of being alive by their command of the symbols of life itself. Even they fail to arc the meaning of their words to all others—M.L. King to Bull Connor, for example.

Now. I have taken onto myself the mantle of writer. As a writer I come from my feelings, from the images which my feelings evoke and when I want you to know what I am experiencing in thought and feeling I form words in patterns, poems, essays. I seek to say that which is so for me. I seek to energize those feelings and thoughts which are the highest expression of who I am and who we are, and to share them. For what purpose? To create with all others a civilization of Highly Evolved Beings.

Such a civilization is possible, you know. It is be-able, one by one, by each of us. Thus it is do-able, cluster by cluster, by segments of us; thus it is experience-able by all of us on this spiritual threshold we are privileged to share.

What Is To Be Done?

This is one of those times when the question "What is to be done?" hovers, spoken and unspoken, where we stand. You and I, the family, the neighborhood, the company, the town, the state, the nation, the world and all the ethnic, political, religious groups and sub-groups that make up our human environment are experiencing severe social turbulence and the question, for sure, is "What is to be done?"

More often than not this question gives rise to a search for and discovery of what is wrong. Listing all the things that are wrong seems to call forth, then, the question of who did it. Who is to blame? That being accomplished, great adversarial energies are called upon and verbal war is often followed by actual combat. Combatants are notoriously forgetful of what it is that they are killing each other for, except, of course, "He hit me first!" Often, in order to keep hating and engaging in fratricide we are exhorted to "Remember the Alamo" or "Preserve the lifestyles of the Kuwaiti sheiks" or "Remember the Maine"—or Pearl Harbor or one massacre or another, always in the past. Thus we have described the mean-spirited arena which American politics has become, to say nothing of the ethnic turmoil erupting world wide.

For my purposes here, I propose that we drop the search for what is wrong. Instead I would ask, "What is it that, being accomplished, would most please me and my family and my company and my neighborhood and my city and my state and my nation and the world community? What would bring to all the most satisfaction, even joy?" I suppose that such a question brought to, say, a committee of peers, or perhaps, elders, would produce quite a list. I propose that the very act of compiling such a list by people of wisdom and good will would evoke a remarkable upsurge of creative energies and would give rise to investment of time, energy and capital toward a much more people friendly world.

But still, though its context might change in seismic measure, the question "What is to be done?" will challenge us. "What is to be done?" is a threshold question. Always the question invites us to step forward into new context. I would listen for what it is that the questioner is attending to, looking at, seeing as going on, that prompts the question, "What is to be done?" We are learning that thought precedes perception. What we are looking for is what we see. Or, as someone, Wayne Dyer I think, put it, "What you believe is what you see." Or, could we say, "Believing is seeing"?

I think a good case can be made for that. A person whose belief system includes a prejudgment of an individual or an ethnic or religious group tends to perceive only that which supports the prejudice. It is as though he carries with him a basket into which he gathers experiential data that matches the data already collected and he simply does not perceive any conflicting data.

And the basket gets heavier and heavier and the burdened one gets more and more resentful, until, boom!, we have Sarajevo, Beirut, Belfast, the American inner city and politics as we know it today. Add to that the increasing incidence of family violence and divorce.

Interesting! How is it that whenever this kind of conversation gets under way we tend to collectively put together a picture composed of things which are wrong, things we perceive as needing to be fixed. We set up a base from which we function much as though we were prejudiced. Into our baskets go our perceptions of what is wrong. What I want to do here is get us out of these fruitless entanglements with the past.

Consider this. In dozens of major cities each day thousands of automobiles converge. They pour in on freeways and expressways and the only possible way that this is accomplished with so little death and mayhem is the daily miracle brought about by thousands of individual drivers, who, by choice, watch out for each other and move in a cadence and rhythm that works. Daily, they manage to do the right thing. Of course we must acknowledge the existence of a minority of drivers who, through ignorance or stupidity or emotional disturbance and insanity, disrupt the flow and cause whatever death and damage that does occur. But, again, consider the miracle of good citizenship and courtesy that normally occurs.

Then how about this question? What is to be done that will result in the expansion into the other areas of our society of the common decency and common sense that the vast majority of drivers manifest every day of the year? And what is to be done that will result in the education of the ignorant, the training and/or the limitation of the right to drive of the stupid, and the healing of the emotionally disturbed and insane, and thus their return to the privileges of freedom to drive and to live among us?

What Is To Be Done?

Well, try this for starters. First we acknowledge the system as miraculously workable by sane and experienced individuals of good will. Then we deliberately identify those who are messing up the system and work with them and for them until they are able to participate as miracle drivers, too. Until then they must be kept out of the drivers' seats. This deprives them of the right to keep the system from working. Yes, and this provides a method and an opportunity to bring about the individual self-determined transformation of dysfunctional drivers.

Good. That's a start. Now we can look together to other opportunities to be attended to. It would be optimum to acknowledge what works and expand on that. In the process of doing that we naturally uncover that which is dysfunctional and work on that toward transformation. But the context for this transformation is not fixing that which is wrong but adding to and enhancing that which is working.

Specters

This cold morning is the end of a week when the air temperature seldom went above zero Fahrenheit. The forecast is for another week of it ahead of us. We humans here live in a miracle cocoon of shelter, heat and light, hot and cold running water, and waste water discharge. Each house is a tiny infrastructure essential to civilization. Each home is a civilization dependent on a system of organization of activities and processes outside the home. Should those systems and processes break down the civilization would tend to break down. What would we families do in this zero weather if our heating system broke down and the lights went out and the incoming water and the wastewater discharge froze and stopped functioning? What if our cars wouldn't work for lack of fuel so we couldn't bundle up and head south? What if our money became useless and we couldn't buy anything? What if this were a nationwide breakdown of the infrastructure? A worldwide breakdown? What would all of our Homo sapiens do, dependent as they are on each other for making the systems and processes work—systems and processes which in this scenario are not working.

Actually, this is a scenario which exists for some alienated and isolated people even now. This is a scenario which can exist in a very short time span in the north and south frigid zones of our small planet. And even in the temperate and tropic zones the time frame for the survival of the Homo sapiens would only be a bit longer. They would starve in days, or weeks or months of time as millions are doing, even now. They would not freeze in days or hours as would happen here.

There is a considerable literature available now that describes this kind of breakdown here in our comfortable world. The scenarios are postulated in terms ranging from possibility to probability to inevitability. This has become part of our conversation and is forming as a fearful specter of what-if in the background of our thinking. This specter easily is linked to the memories and stories of the depression of the thirties and becomes palpably real in the so-called smokestack centers which have shut down in recent years, focussing the attention of thousands to the thrall of slow disaster. And thrall is a good word for it. We become bonded to these specters formed in our conversation. They take on increasing depth and reality whether by our embracing them or by our ignoring them. Karl Marx wrote that there was a "specter haunting Europe, the specter of communism." Indeed. And that specter has taken on more and more reality during the 140 years since he wrote that. What I am saying here is that there is a specter haunting mankind now, and that specter is that of breakdown and disaster.

Let me say right now that specters are created by human being. Specters take form in the conversation of human being. Specters become operationally real and can be experienced as they are energised and acted out by human being. They take on that energy by way of the conversation of human being. As our conversation goes, so go our specters. As our specters take on reality our conversation becomes more and more the product of thralldom to that reality. There are times in history when the specters had most of mankind enthralled. I think of Nazi Germany and the wars promulgated in the thrall of that specter-become-flesh. I think of the Great Depression; I think of Northern Ireland, of Lebanon, of the Palestine situation. I think of the monstrosities of racism, of CIAs and GPUs, of Sandinistas and Contras and gangsters and—on and on. Specter-driven, all!

As a rule, specters do not form in the conversation of human being from nothing. They take form from the observation of things going on in the world. Things going on in the world are the result of caused motions initiated by human being which, usually, except in the case of criminals and psychotics, are attempts to solve observed problems and are well intentioned and mean no harm. The specter begins to take shape when human-caused motions are considered harmful, or wrong or sinful or contra-survival to the observer. A case begins to be made.

An image is created which is used to show to others verbally that the promulgator's intentions were not good, that harm would result from the caused motion. Almost immediately the attention is drawn away from the caused motion itself to opinions and assertions about the motion, arguments then develop and, by this process a caused motion is given form as a specter and a new enthrallment begins.

Caused motions can be dealt with, in motion, in respectful human communication. Kahlil Gibran said, "A divided house is not a den of thieves, it is only a divided house." Caused motions can be seen quite accurately as game activity—human beings operating via their Homo sapiens on this planetary playing field. The specters of enemies, of evil ones, of conspiracies and accusations, of intended harm, are something else again. Human beings enthralled by the specters they have created are not free to play the game in motion. Instead they must act out the specter dance, almost always to the harm of one another.

There are specters haunting our small and lovely world. There is the specter of criminals vs. police, the specter of communism vs. capitalism, the specter of nuclear disaster, the specter of economic disaster, and religious and "true belief" specters of every stripe and hue. We could say that specters are the isms generated by ists.

If I were to say of a family who lived nearby that they were "doing" drugs and abusing children when the actuality was that they were growing medicinal herbs and were providing a warm and friendly activity center for children, I would be creating the beginnings of a specter. The specter would not take on the power of enthrallment until at least one other citizen bought into my declaration. When someone says that another country or race of people or religious belief system is a harmful threat to the survival of the rest of us, or some of us, and I buy into that declaration though I have never seen actual harm come from those so accused, I am aligning with the creation of a specter. I am adding to the power of a specter to enthrall, to ensnare the attention of others.

Now I hear, "Wait! What about actual villainy in the world? People do break into houses; they actually do harm to other people. There are those who, allowed to operate freely in the world, would soon have us in raging barbarism again."

"Yes," I say. And such as these are inevitably found to be operating in the enthrallment of one or more specters, which are energised by opposition and agreement of one or more others. To modify Pogo's statement, "We have met the enemy and they are our specters."

And from another voice there comes, "Yes, there are gossip specters and criminal specters and poverty specters and wars and rumors of wars, but what of the good specters? What about the belief in, oh, the Brotherhood of Man, the Return of Christ, Divine Healing or Heaven?"

To this voice I say: to the degree that these are specters—beliefs—and not acknowledgements of what is actually seen to be so, beliefs operate as barriers to knowledge of what is actually so.

The voice says, "But everyone operates with a belief system, a cloud of specters in some form or another."

And I say that seems to be so until one day you come across one—and they are here among us—who does not operate in the shadow of any specters at all.

"Does that mean this person is an agnostic or an atheist or a nihilist?" you ask.

And I say, "No, those, too, are specters." I say that such a one is operating from direct knowledge, from certainty, and not from beliefs and other spectral stuff. In addition he is operating now and not in the thrall of the past.

Certainty is the opposite of arrogance. One doesn't need to prove certainty. Being certain does not mean one knows everything. Humility accompanies certainty. From humility one knows that one doesn't know, and is willing to acknowledge that there is always more to be known. Humility and integrity are as one. From certainty, from humility, from integrity, one is content to be silent; and when one speaks, it is with one voice, a voice tuned to the listening. I am willing to declare that certainty and direct knowledge are a life-gift to all of us, ours for our acknowledgement and our practice. Especially practice.

The practice consists of simplicities which can become second nature because these simplicities are life-gifts—given already, ours for the acknowledgement and the practice. They had best not be conceptualized or held onto. So we are looking at non-spectral practice, and I want to make it clear that I am looking along with you.

There is a phrase L. Ron Hubbard used: "Look, don't think." The simplicities of looking and of listening are actions, and these actions precede the complexities of hearing and seeing. We tend to hear and see in the context of our operating specters. When we look and are awake we encounter what is out there. A living tree shows up, and there is actual space between thee and tree. And the space is living space, and you connect—make contact with the livingness of space and tree and thee. Something alive takes place. Try it. Just look. Simply listen. There are many other channels by which human being reaches forth into the physical but, like looking and listening, they are outreaches from awake being. They are the doing of human being in the world, and these outreaches precede the perception of what has been done. And the perception of what has been done almost always takes the familiar form. Yesterday's trees are stored in a sequence of trees that are there when I go out the door of my house. Seasonal changes are noted and wind damage may get recorded when noticed, but the this-here-right-now tree gets lost from direct 3-D contact, complete with sounds and movement; looking gets lost on the flat conceptual screen. We deal then with spectral trees and miss out on what is the aliveness of trees. So non-spectral practice requires that we look, listen, sense temperature changes—feel our own weight as it presses through our feet and meets the resistance of the earth or floor which is other than our own weight.

When I left the warm house and walked out into the cold, I didn't need to do that to be cognizant of the probability that it was indeed cold outside. Such is the usefulness of stored concepts and the monitor on which we approximate our experiences. But I also did not experience what was actually so about that particular cold on that particular morning. I didn't need to, I chose not to, and I acknowledged all of that. Now where does the specter come in? The specter is the product of the monitor, the screen, the filter, the translator out of which comes the "made" reality—reality made from altered data, data altered to conform with previously altered data, all of which is declared to be what was perceived. And quickly believed to be what was perceived. The specter is formed from data collected from experience and from the human conversation ongoing. And its form is contrived, and its relationship to what is so is only just sufficient to make it buyable and sellable in the spectral marketplace.

So we have a cold day outside. We can perceive it is cold from visual perception, from the cycling of the furnace, from the news reports. We do not have to experience the cold itself. We can use the mechanisms from which specters are made to act in a survival manner without making or adding to specters. And we can make and add to cold specters—as in, "My God it's cold! Brrrrr! You'll catch your death!" and so on. Specters, taken lightly, can be kind of fun. They add drama to our conversation. Problems arise, however, when we whomp up or buy into conversational specters we don't identify as such.

We have a mental mechanism, part of our created equipment as human being, that is useful for approximating what is going on so that one can have a model to work with, to "what-if," with multitudes of possibilities arising from observed motion. We have a tool—call it our conceptualizer, or our approximator—call it our memory, for that is what it is. All that is required for its appropriate use is that we be aware of the distinction between approximated motion, concepts about what is so, and motion itself, that which actually is so. It is a good and useful tool. Like any tool it can be misused. What is important here is that we be aware that we have and use this tool. And along with that awareness we must recognize that its use without awareness can result in a manufactured reality that takes on a conceptualized "life" of its own, a specter.

0-595-30028-6